*Love,
Dr. Scipio*

D0831683

Let Babies Teach

Learning Child Development
Through Observing Infants and Toddlers

Dr. Vonda K. Scipio

Endorsements

"This book provides a broad and practical introduction to educators/caregivers who work with infants and toddlers. Its strong and insightful coverage of infant/toddler development comes from children's perspectives. This engaging writing style helps readers to understand and promote the essential skills, knowledge, and dispositions required to work with infants and toddlers. I look forward to using this book for my infant/toddler development course at the University of Memphis."

Satomi Izumi-Taylor, Ph.D.
Professor of Early Childhood Education
Youth Services Program Coordinator
The University of Memphis, Memphis, TN

"This is a must read for every new parent. It is written in an easy to read format and is a guide for parents' understanding of the growth and development of their child's critical years from infant through toddler. The companion guide in Part Two has wonderful activities, songs, and rhymes for new parents to interact and engage their babies and toddlers in an easy and entertaining way. It is a guide the entire family can use to help the baby to thrive and develop."

Kay Reeves, Ed.D.
Clinical Associate Professor/Special Education
The University of Memphis, Memphis, TN

"Dr. Scipio's book offers new parents so much important information in a very accessible format. In addition to providing information, parents are given activities for participation in their child's development. There are pages for the readers to record their thoughts and charts for tracking their child's development. This book will serve to instill confidence in parents and to give babies a great start. Every new parent should own a copy."

Joan Kastner, Ph.D.
Executive Director of Special Education and Literacy
Kean University, Union, NJ

"Dr. Vonda Scipio has done the world a favor by calling attention to early childhood experiences and parenting. She has put together a tool that will allow any parent or professional educator to gain insight on how to support a developing mind. She provides a wealth of knowledge from personal collaborations, experiences, and field work that will guide any parent and professional to create a nurturing environment that is conducive for the development of any young child. Early experiences affect the quality of establishing either a sturdy or fragile foundation for children. Dr. Scipio has created a tool that allows parents and professionals to ensure that all children develop a sturdy foundation."

Divalyn L. Gordon, EdS
Former Principal, Ridgeway Early Learning Center
Current Principal, Raleigh-Bartlett Meadows Elementary School
Shelby County Schools
Memphis, TN

Foreword

Let Babies Teach: Learning Child Development through Observing Infants and Toddlers is a delightful and ingenious way to learn about the growth and development of infants and toddlers—through the eyes and voice of babies. Mothers and other caregivers (fathers, grandmothers, babysitters, and professional child development workers) will not only learn about the milestones of child development in each of the major areas of development, including physical, cognitive, social and emotional, but they will also learn from the child the kinds of activities in which they (mothers) should engage the baby that will assist in advancing growth of the child to the next stage of development. A special feature written into this book is space for the mother to record the skills that the baby is developing in each of the development areas and concerns that she may have that will serve as a record when consulting with the pediatrician during regular visits and other specific visits required for immediate medical assistance. These opportunities for reflections on the growth and development of the infant /toddler serve as important developing records of the baby's development that will be useful in the months and years that follow.

Part two of this guide, *Let Me Teach You, Baby: How to Help Infants and Toddlers Grow and Develop Literacy Skills,* includes a wealth of activities and resources that parents and other caregivers can use to further develop important literacy skills for infants and toddlers. Both sections of this guide will not only be an insightful and easy-to-read resource for mothers and other caregivers, but will serve as an important text for graduate and undergraduate students enrolled in infant and toddler courses and professionals who serve as teachers and administrators in child development programs.

This two-volume guide, *Let Babies Teach: Learning Child Development through Observing Infants and Toddlers* and *Let Me Teach You, Baby: How to Help Infants and Toddlers Grow and Develop Literacy Skills,* is a significant contribution both to the practical application of child development concepts for mothers and other caregivers and for professionals in the field of early childhood education.

Vivian Gunn Morris, Ph.D.
Professor of Education (Retired)
College of Education
University of Memphis

Dr. Morris has co-authored the following books: *The price they paid: Desegregation in an African American community, Creating caring and nurturing educational environments for African American children, Child care in a family setting: A comprehensive guide to family day care,* and *Family life and human sexuality.* Her co-authored articles have appeared in several refereed journals including: *Childhood Education, Early Childhood Education Journal, International Journal of Early Childhood, Journal of Teacher Education, Action in Teacher Education, Teaching and Teacher Education, British Journal of In-service Education,* and the *University of Florida Journal of Law and Public Policy.*

Dedications

> "Free the child's potential and you will transform him (her) into the world."
>
> —Maria Montessori

Hi, Grandpop,

Your daughter carried me, a newborn infant, up the back stairwell of the hospital to sneak me in to see and be held by you. I know what you told me. You told me I was beautiful and how proud you were to be my grandpop. You told me I was smart and that I would read and write many books. From infancy, you spoke my potential into existence.

You only had a third-grade education, but you inspired your daughter to get a bachelor's degree and your granddaughter (me) to get a doctorate degree. Your daughter read to me as many books as the library would allow her to check out. She did this long before I could read and get my own library card. We made many trips to the library because I just couldn't get enough of all those fascinating stories. I liked the way she changed her voice for the characters. Her arms were always so soft, and she smelled so good. I didn't know at the time that I couldn't read because after she would read me the book, she would then hand it to me and say, "Read the book to Mommy." She was just as fascinated with my reading as I was with hers.

Your son-in-law, my dad, engaged me in higher-order thinking just like she did. I saw him read countless books. He even read the dictionary, not just to look up words he didn't know; he read it like a book. He taught me to think, analyze, and reflect. He engaged me in conversations, elicited my opinion, and made me feel strong and smart in my gender. One of the greatest lessons he taught me, through word and example, was "self-control." The consistent practice and refinement of this skill has allowed me to accomplish great things in life.

At family gatherings, all the adults would gather around and encourage me to tell the story of Chicken Little. I was always excited to tell about how the sky was falling and Chicken Little was off to tell the king. As a four-year-old, I thought that my audience enjoyed the story as much as I did. As an adult, I realized that they not only enjoyed the story but they were preparing me for my incredible future. Just like you, Grandpop, they were validating me and speaking my potential into existence.

You didn't live long after our meeting. Grandpop, I have already read thousands of books. This is the first one that I have written, and it is dedicated to you.

Thank you, Grandpop, for your legacy. Grandpop, you and I will change the world together, and through us, all families of the earth will be blessed.

Love,

Your granddaughter—Dr. Scipio

Chester Butler, December 29, 1898-September 21, 1967

> "Certainly, parents play a crucial role in the lives of individuals who are intellectually gifted or creatively talented. But this role is not one of active instruction, of teaching children skills... rather, it is support and encouragement parents give their children and the intellectual climate that they create in the home which seem to be critical factors."
>
> —David Elkind

Dearest Mom and Dad,

Where do I begin? I begin with gratitude for your precious gift of parenting. You shared with me that you didn't know all the areas of child development, but you did know the Master who developed me. You shared how you depended on him for guidance in how to raise my siblings and me. My spiritual development was the most important part of my development to you, and you used this knowledge to guide my behavior.

Well, as I review all the child development checklists, you did a marvelous job. I can say this with pride. My outlook and approach to life are directly connected to how you developed me in the areas of language, physical, cognitive, social-emotional, and self-help development during my early childhood years. You challenged me intellectually in every area of development. Whenever I got to one level, you raised it.

Thank you for introducing me to the village, all the neighbors, library workers, store clerks, teachers, lunchroom attendants, secretaries, administrators, public safety personnel, church workers, morticians, postal

To the Reader

The reader is expressly warned to consider and adopt all safety precautions for the activities herein to avoid all potential hazards. The reader willingly assumes all risks regarding suggested activities.

This book is also not intended to substitute for the advice of your pediatrician or other physician who should be consulted on infant and toddler matters, especially if your child shows any sign of illness or unusual behavior.

As of this printing, the website URLs referenced herein were accurate. However, due to the fluid nature of the Internet, we cannot guarantee their accuracy for the life of the edition.

A Special Thanks

Thank you to all the families in Memphis, Germantown, and Collierville, TN who allowed me to visit their homes weekly and aid in their children's development. Every visit was designed to further your knowledge of your child. Immediate observational feedback was given as you engaged your children in activities. So, as a "guide on the side" I was never developing your child, you were. Thank all of you who read this book and gave incredible input to improve it. Thank you to all the parents over the course of my career who allowed me to assist them.

A special "thank you" to my marketing team who guided me through the process (Steve Harrison, Rose George, Raia King, Martha Bullen, Geoffrey Berwind, Tamra Nashman, Mary Guissefi, Danette Kubanda, Brian Edmonson, Gail Snyder, S. Renee, Bob Taylor, Carl Bussler, and Jessica Sulaiman) and editor Madalyn Stone.

Dr. Scipio

As I carried my daughter in my womb, the anticipation and planning for her arrival was very exciting. I spent a lot of time envisioning what life would be like with her before she arrived. She was three weeks premature. When I went into labor, I knew that each contraction was preparing us both to finally see each other. Her dad saw her first.

When they placed her in my arms, I can't describe the incredible joy that I felt. I must borrow Stevie Wonder's words, "I never thought through love, my husband and I would be making one as lovely as she." I counted those precious fingers and toes. I kept sniffing that wonderful baby smell. I stared at her to memorize all her features. I introduced myself to her and said, "I'm Mommy."

As she opened her eyes and continued to adjust her vision, I made sure that my face was right there. I requested that they bring her to my hospital room by seven in the morning and return her to the nursery at seven in the evening. This was the maximum time I could have with her. We stayed in the hospital for seven days and got to know each other better each day.

When my husband and mother came to take us home, I cried because they were putting clothes on her, bundling her in a snowsuit and blankets. They stared at me, and I continued to weep as I uttered, "She's going to be too hot." It was the middle of a New Jersey winter. The awesome responsibility of motherhood had taken hold of me, and I was ready to protect her from anybody, even my husband and mother.

I developed a routine for everything. I played, talked, sang, and read to her. My husband and I decided which routines he would have when he came home from work. We were a team. During those infant-toddler years, I was surrounded by older women who observed my parenting and gave input on what I was doing right and areas that needed improvement. I listened and incorporated everything they told me. I would call and ask them questions: my mom, Miss Ruby, Miss Joyce, Miss Anita, Miss Lucy, Miss Chester, and Miss Exzora. These women were concerned about me as a young wife and mother.

Miss Ruby told me to potty train Nicole when she was sixteen months. She told me that Nicole was so prissy that she was not going to like urine running down her legs. She ensured that I transition her to pretty panties and never use diapers again. She gave me all the steps for a successful transition. I prepared Nicole for days and told her about the steps. I put the potty chair together and put her on it. She immediately used it to urinate and make a bowel movement.

I jumped up and down, danced around that potty, clapped, and told her what an amazing little girl she was. I called her dad at work and announced it. I called all her grandparents. Miss Ruby didn't tell me to do this, but I sure saved two of Nicole's first presents in her potty for when her dad arrived home. Ms. Ruby was right; she never had an accident in her panties.

That was a pivotal moment in our relationship. As I cheered and danced around her potty chair, I looked at her. She had a sense of pride on her face that made her look much older and much taller. We locked eyes and realized we both had so much to teach each other and so much to learn from each other. That realization inspired the title of this book, *Let Babies Teach,* and the companion guide, *Let Me Teach You, Baby.*

I have countless amazing stories and memories of my daughter's infant and toddler years. I was always observing and preparing her for the next phase. Her dad and I engaged her in language, cognitive, physical, social-emotional, and self-help skills development. Guiding her behavior was important to maintain balance in all other areas of development. I constantly assessed my own emotional state, behavior, and development as a parent in all the areas.

I have worked in the field of early childhood education for a total of twenty-eight years, ever since I took my daughter to her toddler Thursday night Bible class and asked the minister if I could assist with teaching the class. I have assisted hundreds of families over the course of my career. I was fortunate to be a stay-at-home mom until it was time to send her off to kindergarten, where I volunteered in her classroom. I finally had to let her go in first grade, but you can believe I was there for the daily morning exercises that they had for the children and parents. You can also believe I was there to pick her up when the bell rang. I knew her principal, teachers, and other educational workers and partnered with them to make all our jobs easier.

I also knew my daughter's classmates and their parents, and we all engaged our children in higher-learning and extracurricular activities. I believed in the home/school connection, and it worked. Her dad couldn't leave work for every event, so I updated him when he arrived home. He gave input and suggestions for me to share with the school that made the home/school connection even more meaningful. That home/school connection lasted throughout her high school years. My former husband and I were truly my daughter's first teachers, and the teachers at school were her second teachers.

That young lady who changed the trajectory of my life from woman to mother is still as precious to me today as she was when I first laid eyes on her. She is now the amazing mother of my two very precious three- and five-year-old grandsons. I never knew love like this! I am still her mother, and now I'm their Mema as well.

I have focused on early childhood education throughout my career and have found this work very rewarding. All children have potential, but it is up to capable adults to bring it out. I have eighteen years of experience as an independent early childhood consultant, adjunct professor, trainer, advisor, parent educator, kindergarten teacher, early intervention specialist, and supervisor/ trainer of early intervention specialists. I advocate for children and their families in my work with colleges, universities, councils, resource and referral agencies, quality improvement centers, state agencies, boards of education, school districts, administrators, child care centers, private companies, churches, teachers, parents, and most of all, with amazing children. Everything I do in my career is to ensure I make this world better for them.

I studied to get a bachelor's and master's degree so I would be prepared. I earned the New Jersey Teacher N-8 and Trainer Certifications, along with the Highest Achievement Award from the Dale Carnegie Course to support my ability to train children and adults. My greatest satisfaction came from earning my doctorate in education with a focus on instruction and curriculum leadership and a concentration in early childhood.

For the past six years, I have gone home with infants, toddlers, and their families to provide coaching and training. Over one hundred families have received guidance and support. I have worked as a "guide on the side" for parents by strengthening their parenting skills to be "potential driven." They became better positioned to assist their children in reaching their developmental milestones. Homes were rich when I arrived and were even richer for my being there. My findings showed that each family needed assistance in its knowledge of child development.

I am still here and plan on working with many more families. This handbook is a culmination of my life's work with children and families in the home and in institutions that serve them. It is written for children with typical development that lies within the normal or average range, as well as for children with atypical development that lies outside the normal or average range. Those who serve children need to understand child development to know when infants and toddlers are expected to gain certain skills. This knowledge provides a basis for parents and caregivers to understand and meet the needs of infants and toddlers.

This handbook covers the five domains of early childhood development: language (receptive and expressive), physical (gross and fine motor), cognitive (thinking and responding), social-emotional, and self-help. Each chapter provides certain skill sets unique to a specific area of development. Some chapters include development activities. Each developmental domain includes an assessment that is specific to the domain and information covered in the chapter. Each chapter has a development assignment. There is also an additional chapter on guiding behavior. The handbook has been written in a child's voice. It is educational, humorous, and inspirational. Part 2 of this handbook includes a delightful companion guide, *Let Me Teach You, Baby*, to help parents and caregivers further develop important literacy skills for infants and toddlers. The guide includes fun photos and engaging poems.

Because I cannot make it to everyone's home or every institution, I wrote this handbook to assist you and to be a source of guidance. It will not only enable you to be your child's first teacher, it will also help you understand and nurture your child. Thank you for making me part of the team.

Let's get started!

Dr. Scipio

Preface

I wanted to write a book to help parents and caregivers of infants and toddlers understand child development. I also wanted to empower them to be their child's first teacher. Some parents are waiting until their children get to school for the "real learning" to begin. Some parents view teachers as experts, but some teachers don't view parents in the same light. When parents arrive at the school with their children, some educators seem to say, "I'll take it from here." Some parents seem to say, "Here, educate my child for me." During my trainings with educators, they shared that "parents just don't get it." Whenever I coached parents, they shared that "teachers just don't understand." The gap needs to be bridged between "not getting it" and "not understanding."

During my career, I analyzed that educators and parents don't use the same terminology for child development domains. Educators use the terms "language" or "communication development"; parents call it "speech" or "talk." Educators use the term "physical development" ("gross and fine motor"); parents call it "movement" and "picking up things." Educators use the term "cognitive development"; parents call it "thinking" or "learning." Educators use the term "social-emotional"; parents call it "feelings" and "sharing." Educators use the term "self-help" or "adaptive development"; parents call it "potty training" or "doing things independently." Also, educators and parents don't have the same set of skills needed in each domain or the expected time frames of mastery. The educators needed list of skills is much more comprehensive. All parents must be equipped and empowered with the knowledge of how and when to teach their children developmental skills. The challenges experienced by children, parents, and teachers often combine to create a perfect storm in which each blames the other. This book was written to assist with this dilemma.

Consequently, while doing therapy in their homes, I was also able to analyze the recurring developmental challenges faced by parents. The challenges faced by parents are proportional to the challenges faced by teachers in achieving the state learning standards. Some of the common skills of development, in which children are engaged across homes, are included in this handbook. Instead of writing from an academic standpoint, it was written from the child's perspective.

Furthermore, my expertise in early childhood education enables me to see the perspective of educators, parents, and children. My perspective is further enhanced from being a parent, grandparent, and an educator. I was engaged in these principles by my own parents. The skills in which I engaged my daughter from birth continue to be used for my own grandchildren and the families I serve. Observing from the child's perspective will provide a better understanding of the principles of child development.

This book provides a training tool for parents, caregivers, and educators to better equip them in their roles as teachers. It will also shed light on the need for teamwork between the home and school. Educating and empowering parents, caregivers, teachers, and children within the walls of homes and schools will bridge the connection between home and school and better prepare children in their academic pursuits. This book is designed to focus the reader on timeless child development principles of infants and toddlers. Let's allow these infants and toddlers to lead us as a nation, state, city, community, and home.

The companion guide, *Let Me Teach You, Baby: How to Help Infants and Toddlers Grow and Develop Literacy Skills,* was written to empower parents and caregivers to engage children in early literacy from birth. It was written in the adult's voice in response to *Let Babies Teach.*

How to Use this Book

1. There is a required early childhood education research assignment at the end of each chapter. There will be quotes throughout this handbook from early childhood pioneers. Please add your thoughts after reading each quote. Please research each pioneer to learn about his or her contribution to the field of early childhood education.

2. Read each chapter of this book and reflect on your current practices with your infants and toddlers.

3. After reading each chapter, complete the assessment.

4. There will also be a required development assignment for chapters 2-7. Please review the listed websites to learn more about your child's development. Please choose recommended strategies to add to your list of development activities. Review the milestones directly before your child's age, age range, and beyond your child's age range. Review each age range for each developmental area: language, physical gross/fine motor, cognitive, social-emotional, and self-help. Example: If your child is 12 months, review the milestones for 9-12, 12-15, and 15-18 months so that you will know what to expect.

5. Age ranges are listed throughout the chapters. There are no charts listed in this book because development occurs at various rates depending on biology and engagement.

6. Enjoy engaging your infants and toddlers in development.

"Each of us must come to care about everyone else's children. We must recognize that the welfare of our children and grandchildren is intimately linked to the welfare of all other people's children. After all, when one of our children needs lifesaving surgery, someone else's child will perform it. If one of our children is threatened or harmed by violence, someone else's child will be responsible for the violent act. The good life for our own children can be secured only if a good life is also secured for all other people's children."

—Lillian Katz

Your Thoughts:

"If the children and youth of a nation are afforded opportunity to develop their capacities to the fullest, if they are given the knowledge to understand the world and the wisdom to change it, then the prospects for the future are bright. In contrast, a society which neglects its children, however well it may function in other respects, risks eventual disorganization and demise."

—Urie Bronfenbrenner

Your Thoughts:

Introduction

> "Children need people in order to be-
> come human...It is primarily through
> observing, playing, and working with
> others older and younger than him-
> self that a child discovers both what he
> can and who he can become—that he
> develops both his ability and his iden-
> tity...Hence to relegate children to a
> world of their own is to deprive them of
> their humanity, and ourselves as well."
> —Urie Bronfenbrenner

What is done with me in the upcoming minutes, hours, days, months, and years is going to make or break me. I am clay and need you to be a potter. There is no requirement to attend potter school, and a potter's wheel is not always provided. I must be created using the right balance of language (receptive and expressive), physical (gross and fine motor), cognitive (thinking and responding), social-emotional, and self-help development. Guiding my behavior is the key to successfully engaging me in all areas of development. This awesome charge has been given to you. There is no training. There is no course to take, no certificate to obtain, and no licensure. Titles have been given because of my birth. There are no other qualifications.

There is another area of my development that is often overlooked—spiritual development. My "spirit" is the inner force that gives me life, energy, and power. There is another Potter that can be partnered with to assist with my development and feed my spirit. That Potter already introduced himself to me as God while I was in the womb. I already know him. Various religions have different names for him, and some consider "him" to be a "her." Whatever spiritual practice is chosen, use it to feed my spirit. It will make my life more meaningful and fill a part of me that nothing else can. If there is no belief in God and a spiritual practice is not chosen, there is still an obligation to engage me in all the other areas of development.

Neither the materials used nor the environment in which I am guided or assisted in my development are taken into consideration during the process. Neither ethnicity nor age is a consideration. Religious affiliation or lack thereof is not considered. Neither education level nor family makeup—good parents, bad parents, no parents, grandparents, or a single parent—are considered. The home I'm taken to when I leave the hospital is also not considered: mansion, house, apartment, trailer, shack, or homeless.

None of these things matter, yet all these things matter. Unlimited resources and support will not guarantee that I successfully reach adulthood, while limited resources and support will not guarantee that I don't successfully reach adulthood. It is the utilization of the resources, limited or unlimited, along with goals that can help me become a responsible, caring adult so I can take my rightful place in society.

This handbook has been compiled to serve as a source of instruction. It will serve as the potter's wheel. It will enable you to mold me, shape me, and understand me. It will also assist in making me into an incredible, smart, caring, compassionate, and empathetic person who will find lasting purpose in life and do all I was created to do.

Remember that my gratification needs to be delayed. I should not be given everything one wants me to have or that I request. Many times, the answer must be "No." My response to "No" needs to be monitored and corrected as necessary. I need to be taught to be grateful for everything done for me to aid in my development. I need to be taught to say thank you. I will, in turn, learn to say thank you to others. I must be taught to do nice things for others without any expectation of reward.

With you as the potter, me as the clay, and this handbook serving as the wheel, there is nothing that cannot be done. This first handbook will assist you in the first three years of my life. There will be more child development handbooks in the future.

At times, there will be the temptation to only provide me with custodial care: food, clothing, and shelter. I need more than this. My television viewing should be limited to educational and children's programs such as *Sesame Street*. This needs to be done in moderation. I have more fun engaging with others and my toys. Cell phone use should be limited when engaging with me. Be in the moment! Be present! Be fully present!

The focus needs to be on every area of my development: language (receptive and expressive), physical (gross and fine motor), cognitive (thinking and responding), social emotional, and self-help. Each area of development needs to be studied individually and then placed back with the others. They need to be taken apart again and placed next to each other, on top of each other, and interspersed with each other. Then I need to be taken and placed amid what was just studied. There are connections. I have strengths. I have weaknesses. Most of all, I have potential. This knowledge needs to be used to help me to develop. My life depends on it. Let's begin!

"We now recognize that abuse and neglect may be as frequent in nuclear families as love, protection, and commitment are in nonnuclear families."

—David Elkind

Your Thoughts:

"In the United States, it is now possible for a person eighteen years of age, female as well as male, to graduate from high school, college, or university without ever having cared for, or even held, a baby; without ever having comforted or assisted another human being who needed help... No society can long sustain itself unless its members have learned the sensitivities, motivations, and skills involved in assisting and caring for other human beings."

—Urie Bronfenbrenner

Your Thoughts:

"We have a great deal to teach infants and toddlers, but right now, let us read this handbook and learn from them."

—The Author

"If a child lives with approval, he learns to live with himself."

—Dorothy Nolte

Your Thoughts:

Chapter 1

Personality Development

Personality development considers the temperament types of children and how they remain surprisingly constant throughout life (Martin & Berke, 2007).

I will be born with a *personality*. This is my overall disposition or temperament. I may be active and intense or relatively slow moving. I may be timid with new experiences or engage with enjoyment. I may be easy-going or easily upset. There will be habitual patterns that I will use to behave and show emotion. If my personality is outgoing and I get energy from interacting with people and objects, I will be labeled as an *extrovert*. These tendencies will be noticeable from infancy. When adults or children get near me, I will get very excited, coo, babble, and smile. I might be the first to elicit the interaction. As a toddler, when I arrive at the park to interact with my play group, I will immediately go over to the children already involved in play and begin to interact with them.

If my personality is more reserved and I get energy from concepts and ideas, I will be labeled as an *introvert*. When adults or children get near me, I might not readily coo, babble, or smile. As they make those funny sounds, faces, and gestures, I might continue to study with an intense look or look away without engagement, while hoping they will leave me alone. As a toddler, when I arrive at the park to interact with my play group, I will wait, observe, and not want to join the group right away. Please study my responses to stimuli from birth. You will see certain preferences begin to emerge as I develop.

There will be a tendency for you to think that "I'm a little you." I'm not; I am a distinct person. Even though I may exhibit some or most of your traits, you will encourage my optimum development by treating me as an individual. Whatever personality I arrive into this world with, please nurture and guide me. Be very careful if you are an extrovert and I am an introvert or vice versa. You might be tempted to make me into your preferred personality style. This will not work. If you do this, we will have conflict in our relationship. Neither personality style is better than the other. Please do not attempt to make me the opposite of who I am. If you do this, you will hinder my growth and development and make me insecure.

If I am an extrovert, I will enjoy the energy of interacting with people. Placing me into situations where

I am alone or interacting in quiet activities may frustrate me. If I am an introvert, I will enjoy the solitude of limited interaction with others and enjoy thinking. The energy of large groups of people may overwhelm me and cause me stress. I need balance in life. Please study my overall disposition and temperament and let me know, through your love and devotion, that I am okay just the way I am. I will then trust you as you engage me in extrovert and introvert activities.

If I am an extrovert and you take me to the park, encourage me to go over to the child who is not playing with the group and engage him or her. Encourage me to entice the child to play with me and with the rest of the group. If the child does not want to join the larger group, encourage me to play with the child for a few minutes by ourselves. Encourage me to make my own decision of whether I want to continue to engage one-on-one with this child or join the larger group. If I am an introvert and you take me to the park, encourage one of the outgoing children to come over and meet me. Encourage the child to spend a few minutes to get to know what I like. Allow me to decide if I want to engage with this child one-on-one or go over and join the group. These are a few examples of engagement activities.

Observe my personality style in relation to all the areas of development: language (receptive and expressive); physical (gross and fine motor); cognitive (thinking and responding); social-emotional; and self-help. This knowledge will assist you as you teach and nurture me. As you learn my preferred personality style, please study other activities that will engage me in both styles. Life requires activities in both arenas. Engaging me in both will prepare me for a balanced life where I will be able to undertake tasks and successfully meet the challenges of life. This engagement will also help me to get along better with others.

For more information on how to help me develop my personality, please see the following sources:

American Academy of Pediatrics website

Your Baby's Temperament
https://www.healthychildren.org/English/ages-stages/
baby/Pages/Babys-Temperament.aspx

Emotional and Social Development: 4 to 7 months
https://www.healthychildren.org/English/ages-stages/
baby/Pages/Emotional-and-Social-Development-4-7-
Months.aspx

"The goal of early childhood education should be to activate the child's own natural desire to learn."

—Maria Montessori

Your Thoughts:

"Children must master the language of things before they master the language of words."

—Friedrich Frobel

Your Thoughts:

"The specifically human capacity for language enables children to provide for auxiliary tools in the solution of difficult tasks, to overcome impulsive action, to plan a solution to a problem prior to its execution, and to master their own behavior."

—Les Vygotsky

Your Thoughts:

Chapter 2

Language Development
—Let Me Talk

Communication refers to interactions using visual and sound signals and especially to the acquisition of *language*—the symbolic system of exchanging thoughts and feelings. Language acquisition depends on the child interacting with people and hearing language (Martin & Berke, 2007).

Crying

Thank you for talking, singing, and reading to me while I am in the womb. I hear you. When I arrive into the world, my major form of communication will be my cry. I will focus on others with my eyes. I will coordinate body movements with my cries by moving my arms and legs. Study my cries and body movements. From zero to seven months, I will use various intensities and volume levels of crying to express my needs and wants. Speak kindly to me while meeting my needs and wants. Tell me everything is okay. My ability to stop crying when my needs and wants are met is the beginning of my ability to self-regulate.

Development Activities

Soothe me when I cry. Check to see if I am hungry, wet, tired, bored, or in pain. I will use a different cry for each. Take care of my needs. If I still cry as these needs are being met, rock me or walk with me cradled in your arms. Rub my tummy or my back to ease me. Sing or talk to me as you calm me.

Respond to my cries immediately to help me develop a sense of security. Sometimes, I will cry and you won't be able to soothe me. Do the best you can to comfort me. If the crying begins to make you uneasy, reach out to a relative, neighbor, or friend to help. Please don't ever shake me to stop my crying. This can lead to blindness, brain damage, or even death.

Cooing

I will also add another form of communication to my vocal toolbox, called *cooing*. Listen for my cooing around zero to three months. Oh, isn't it such a sweet sound! I move my mouth, tongue, and lips and begin to experiment with vowel sounds: *oo*, *ah*, and *ee*. I coordinate my coos, eye contact, smiles, and head movements and make them all work in unison. Don't I look adorable when I'm cooing? You and others look good to me, too. I will laugh aloud very soon. I like the responses to my coos—smiles, nodding heads, coos, and the strange sounds that I heard in the womb. I think they are called *words*.

Take turns with me: talk, wait for my coo response; talk, wait for my coo response. After singing the song, "You Are My Sunshine," multiple times, sing the first line and wait for my coo response. I will coo the second line and then wait for your response. We will sing/coo the entire song. Please capture this on video because I will find it hard to believe that I did this if you tell me that I did when I am all grown up. Mix words and coos at times to make a connection with me. I won't be introduced to wonderful words if you coo the entire conversation. I will eventually say words, but right now, I am going to get my "coo" on.

Development Activities

Look in my eyes when you talk to me. Check that I am looking at your face and eyes. Please provide me with visual and auditory stimulation (mobile, rattle, or music box). Talk to me with a calm, soothing voice. When I smile or coo in response to your talking, pat me and smile. Continue to talk to me until I respond with a coo or a smile. Please do not make sounds when I am "cooing." Your voice will cause me to stop. I need to practice my first "baby talk."

Please talk to me about the chores you are doing. Please tell me about the sounds that I hear. Use rattles and music boxes to ensure that I can hear. Shake the rattle a few inches from my ear and I will turn to see it. When reading or singing, pause and wait for my coo response.

Squealing

My vocal chords are getting stronger. I am going to add squeals that will delight your soul from two to six months.

Whoa, that first squeal scared me! I like that big smile you just gave me. I'm going to squeal again. Now you're laughing. I'm going to squeal louder. Hey, I'm now getting my "squeal" on!

Development Activities

Make sure I am comfortable, dry, and fed. While you are dressing, bathing, or playing with me, speak kindly to me. Kiss me, hold me tight, and snuggle. Laugh with me and listen to me squeal. When I am alone in my crib and playing with a toy, I may coo, gurgle, laugh, and squeal. When reading an exciting story to me, pause and wait for my squeal. If we have been separated for a while, approach me slowly, smile, and say my name. I will watch your expression and listen to your voice. I will kick, wiggle my body, and squeal with excitement. I missed you.

Babbling and Jabbering

Listen—I am now babbling. Don't talk over me. Allow me to get my "babble" on, and then respond. Teach me to take turns like in regular conversations. Talk, wait for my babble response; talk, wait for my babble response. Copy my babble, but also use words as I use my babble. If only babble is used in this exchange, I won't be introduced to the wonderful words I am going to eventually use.

I will begin to combine syllables: *da-da, ba-ba*, and *ma-ma*. I can now produce consonant sounds (such as *k, g, b, d, m*, and *l*) and put these together with the vowel sounds that I already know (*oo, ee*, and *ah*). I will begin to babble for longer periods. My babble will take on a conversational tone, and I will begin to mix words with babble. The time line for my babble will be 4 to 12 months. At 12 months, I will transition to *jabber*; meaning, I will use my voice in a variety of ways so that the changing volume, pitch, and rhythm sound like real speech.

Development Activities

Place me near a safely mounted mirror or hang a mobile and set it in motion. This will entertain me and inspire me to make talking sounds. When holding, bathing, changing, or playing with me, echo any sounds made by me and interject my baby noises into your conversations. Talk to me and praise me when I attempt to make sounds and verbalize. Please make repeated syllable sounds such as *ma-ma-ma* or *ba-ba-ba*. Encourage me to watch your mouth formations as you speak. Exaggerate the syllables. While reading to me, pause and wait for my babble response.

First Words

I understand many words that I am not yet able to say. This is *receptive language.* Pay special attention to my nonverbal communication in which I use sounds and gestures to indicate what I want and don't want. Please clearly say the word I am trying to use, and I will make attempts to say it, too. Ooh, did you hear my first word? I learn from everyone who talks to me. Make sure I can see everyone's face as they say words. Watch my eye movements to ensure that I am looking at the object you are holding and your mouth. Briefly hold the object up next to your mouth and say the object name. I will look at the object and your mouth. I will imitate lip and jaw movements as I begin to say words. From 12 to 16 months, I will use many single words.

Record my first word and the date in my baby book. I am going to enjoy reading my baby book when I am grown and will also share it with my own children. Record my voice so that I can listen to it now and when I am all grown up. I might say *da-da* before I say *ma-ma*. This is nothing personal, so relax and very soon I will be calling your name so much, you will want to change it.

Oh, look how I can mix words with babble—I'm on

my way! Count the number of words that I say and keep a written record. Look at how fast I'm learning and saying them—this is *expressive language*. I should be using 10 to 15 words spontaneously between 12 and 23 months. Over time, by 24 to 36 months, I will develop a vocabulary of 50 to 300 words. The number of words could increase to 1,000 just before 36 months and beyond. The number of words could vary, and the developmental time frame could be sooner or later, depending on how much and how often I am engaged.

Development Activities

Please show me objects and name them. Ask me what this is and wait for my response. Celebrate any utterance that I make in response to your question. If I don't answer, say the object name and pass it to me. Ask me where an object is, and encourage me to retrieve it. I will begin to say single words and parts of words. I may mispronounce words or miss sounds. I will also mix parts of words with gestures.

While reading, engage me in hand-over-hand pointing as you say object names. I will point at many things in the environment to indicate my needs and wants. Say the words for the items. Whenever you refer to *ma-ma* or *da-da*, use these names. I will soon call each one appropriately.

Two-, Three-, and Four-Word Phrases, Verbs, Adjectives, Pronouns, and Prepositions

What time is it? Oh, it's 24-36 months. Words, words, words—I enjoy using them. One of my favorite words is *no*. I use single words and multiple words and will eventually use two-, three-, and four-word phrases. I use my words to communicate my wants and needs. At this stage, please use sentences when communicating with me. Ask me, "Where are you going?" If I answer in one or two words, then answer the question for me using a complete sentence. Encourage me to repeat, "I am going to the store." Please make it fun, engaging, and natural. If you try to force me, I will stop talking.

I will begin to understand and use verbs, adjectives, pronouns, and prepositions. I will use verbs to describe actions. I may say, "I go'ed to the store" instead of, "I went to the store." After you hear my communication, respond and state it correctly, "Oh, you went to the store." Please don't laugh; celebrate all attempts. I will use adjectives to describe nouns and pronouns. I may say, "My boo shirt" instead of, "My blue shirt." After you hear this, respond, extend, and state it correctly: "You want to wear your blue shirt."

I will use pronouns to take the place of nouns. I may say, "Me want to go" instead of, "I want to go." You should calmly respond, "I want to go." I may repeat it after you or I may repeat, "Me want to go." Do not get into a battle with me; just continue to celebrate my evolving use of language rules. Please teach me prepositions; they show the relationship between nouns, pronouns, and other words in sentences. I will learn the prepositions "in" and "on" before I learn the others. Tell me to put the toy "on" the table. Encourage me to put my toys "in" the tub before bath time.

Some of my words will be intelligible; others will not be. At times, I will become frustrated when I am not understood. Please be patient. I am involved in a language explosion from 12 to 36 months. Use conversations, books, and music to get me going. Before you know it, I will enunciate all words clearly and sing all the words to every song. Please don't say any bad words (you know the words I'm talking about) because I will use them in the proper context and with the correct attitude.

Development Activities

Please teach me how to put words together to make phrases and sentences. For example, if I say, "Want milk," you say, "I want some milk" to show me the correct way to say it.

Act out word meanings. For example, hold me up and say, "You are up high," or put me on the floor and say, "You are down low." Teach me to use my words to indicate my needs and wants. Create your own language games using all the parts of speech and engage me. When reading to me, omit a word and wait for me to say it.

Development Assignment

Please review the following websites to learn more about my language development. Please choose recommended strategies to add to your list of development activities. Review the milestones directly before my age, my age range, and beyond my age range. Example: If I am 12 months, review the milestones for 9-12, 12-15 and 15-18 months, so that you will know what to expect.

American Academy of Pediatrics website

Prenatal
https://www.healthychildren.org/English/ages-stages/prenatal/Pages/default.aspx

Baby
https://www.healthychildren.org/English/ages-stages/baby/Pages/default.aspx

Toddler
https://www.healthychildren.org/English/ages-stages/toddler/Pages/default.aspx

Preschool
https://www.healthychildren.org/English/ages-stages/preschool/Pages/default.aspx

Gradeschool
https://www.healthychildren.org/English/ages-stages/gradeschool/Pages/default.aspx

Developmental Milestones of Early Literacy
https://www.healthychildren.org/English/ages-stages/
baby/Pages/Developmental-Milestones-of-Early-Literacy.
aspx

American-Speech-Language-Hearing Association's website

How Does Your Child Hear and Talk: American Speech-Language-Hearing Association
http://www.asha.org/public/speech/development/chart/

What to Expect website

http://www.whattoexpect.com/milestones/

Zero to Three website

https://www.zerotothree.org/resources/series/your-child-s-development-age-based-tips-from-birth-to-36-months

Language Assessment

Name_____ Age____

Skills

Crying

First Attempt

How Often?

Concerns

Cooing

First Attempt

How Often?

Concerns

Squealing

First Attempt

How Often?

Concerns

Babbling and Jabbering

First Attempt

How Often?

Concerns

First Words

First Attempt

How Often?

Concerns

Two-, Three-, Four- Word Phrases

First Attempt

How Often?

Concerns

Verbs

First Attempt

How Often?

Concerns

Adjectives

First Attempt

How Often?

Concerns

Pronouns

First Attempt

How Often?

Concerns

Prepositions

First Attempt

How Often?

Concerns

Questions for Pediatrician

"Babies control and bring up their families as much as they are controlled by them; in fact, the family brings up baby by being brought up by him."

—Jean Piaget

Your Thoughts:

"Infants and young children are not just sitting twiddling their thumbs, waiting for their parents to teach them to read and do math. They are expending a vast amount of time and effort in exploring and understanding their immediate world. Healthy education supports and encourages this spontaneous learning."

—David Elkind

Your Thoughts:

Chapter 3

Physical Development —Let Me Move

Part 1: Gross Motor Development

Physical development concerns the changes in skill development of the body. The two strands of physical development relate to increasing refinement of control of the large and small muscles of the body. *Gross motor skills* involve control of the large muscles of the body that allow sitting, crawling, walking, and so on. *Fine motor skills* concern the skill development of the smaller muscles that allow for hand control and coordination of hand and eye (Martin & Berke, 2007). This area of development is very extensive and is divided into two chapters—gross motor development is covered in this chapter, and fine motor development is covered in chapter 4.

Tummy Time

Tummy time happens on the floor, not the bed. Create a nice cushioned area on the floor. Make sure the cushion is a flat surface without grooves. Make sure the cushion is thick enough because eventually I will be flipping, turning, and hitting my head as I do this. Start with short tummy time sessions of two minutes and gradually increase the time as I get accustomed to it.

Make sure everything is sanitary because from two and a half to six months, I am going to explore and put everything into my mouth. This is how I learn at this stage of development. Make sure all objects are large enough so that I cannot swallow them. As I place these objects in my mouth, I will learn about textures, shapes, and sizes. I will also learn about the muscles in my mouth and learn to control them as I mouth objects.

Please place me on the floor turned on my tummy for play, and engage me when I am zero to eight months. At first, I'm going to cry as if someone is hurting me. The scream is going to frighten you, and you will not want to put me down there again. Ignore my scream. As you have noticed, since I don't use words, this is my main mode of communication. Pick me up and soothe me. Talk to me about tummy time and encourage me to try it again.

This time, get down there with me so that I can see you. Touch me and name my body parts while engaging me in tummy time. Stretch my arms and legs. As you are on your tummy facing me, dangle my favorite toys in front of me (rattles, toys hanging from mobile, toy keys). I'll be distracted by your wonderful presence and the sheer joy of engaging with you and my favorite toys (soft and washable sensory balls, sight-and-sound tubes, music box). Pass me toys and encourage me to reach for, grasp, and hold them. Place bells on my feet and encourage me to kick. I will learn how to problem solve during tummy time. During tummy time, I will be on my stomach and back. However, remember to place me in the *pediatric recommended* back position for sleeping.

Crawling is a very difficult task. During tummy time, I learn how to do it. Please don't carry me around all the time. If you do, you will carry me the rest of my life because I will lack the independence needed to function without you. Crawling prepares and strengthens my muscles for standing, walking, and climbing. Therefore, I must crawl before I can walk. About 15 percent of typically developing babies walk without crawling first.

Head and Neck Control; Rolling from Side to Back and Back to Side

Place me on my stomach. At first, I won't be able to lift my head. My head is going to be turned to the side against the surface with my left or right ear touching the floor. Talk to me; I'm watching you. Go to the other side—shake those toys and speak kindly. Eventually, as I gain more head and neck control, I'm going to turn my head to that side because I like seeing you. Get in front of me and lift a toy (toy keys, toys that make noise and light up) slightly above my head, and I will push up on my arms and lift my head to see it. This will help me to gain more head and neck control from birth to four months.

Place me on my side and dangle a toy 5-10 inches in front of my eyes. As I watch the toy, move it over my head to the opposite side. Whoa, I just rolled from my side to my back. Do this on both sides. You're clapping? Thank you, thank you. I need more time before I roll from my back to my side—that's a little challenging. Even though it's challenging, get down here with me and engage me by taking my left hand and pulling me to my side. Do this on both sides. Eventually, I will roll from my back to my side without your assistance. Let's do it again; this time, place my favorite toy on my side and shake it. I'm looking at you and the toy. I want that toy; bring it a little closer. I'm going to reach with the hand that's closest to the toy. Now I'm going to bring my other hand over. As I am reaching, by body is turning over. Wow! I'm all the way over on my side and I got the toy. You are amazing and so am I! All of this will occur from birth through four months.

Rolling from Stomach to Back and Back to Stomach

Once I've mastered rolling from my side to my back, it will be easier for me to roll from my stomach to my back. Place my toys strategically to the left, right, above my head, and below my feet just out of reach. I will then pivot on my stomach to engage with each toy. I hear you chuckling as I do this. I must look so cute. This is a great workout.

While on my stomach, place a toy in my line of vision. While I am watching, move yourself and the toy to the side and behind me out of my line of vision. I want that toy and I want you. I am going to tuck one arm under my chest and my back is going to twist in the direction you took that toy. I hear you calling me. I am going to push with my opposite arm and leg and turn over onto my back. Wow! If I don't readily do it, offer me a little assistance. That was great!

Okay, since I got that, I can probably go back over onto my stomach. I just looked into your eyes and noticed a few tears. You are so proud of me, and that pride makes me feel that I can do anything. Let's go! Come over here and lift both of my legs toward my chest. Then help me tilt my hips and legs toward one side, let's start with the right because I'm stronger on that side. I see you placed a toy on the side that I'm facing. Oh, it's Elmo, talking to me. I'm going to reach my arms out to get Elmo. As I am reaching, my body is turning. Thank you for helping me to stretch my legs out when I turned over onto my tummy. Give me a few minutes with Elmo and then let's try my left side. I enjoy being with you. I'm going to turn back onto my stomach without your assistance. Thank you for showing me how. I did it; I turned from my stomach to my back. I want to stay on my back for a little while.

While on my back, watch how I kick my legs and move

my arms. I'm getting ready; these skills are going to come in handy as I grow and develop. These skills prepare me to have more body control needed for sitting, crawling, and standing.

When I am on my tummy, watch how I move my arms and legs and look like an airplane flying in place. Have you considered taking me for swimming lessons? Isn't it amazing how when you pull me into sitting position, my head is now firmly supported by my neck, stays aligned with my body, and doesn't flop to the side? Look for these skills to emerge from four to seven months.

Sitting Assisted

Whoa, all this kicking, moving my arms and legs, and rolling has me ready to sit. How can I sit like you? As you engage me in supported sitting, sit me on your lap and on the floor and hold me at my hips. If I wobble too much, hold me at my hips and waist. Place me on the floor, put toys between my legs, and spread my legs a little. I will begin to engage with the toys and enjoy sitting assisted. I enjoy the security of my back against you as you straddle me between your legs. At first, I'm going to need to have my back against you to sit up straight. Please gradually ease away from me so that my back muscles will be strengthened.

Oh, I feel you letting go as I'm sitting! This causes me to take more control of my body. I must hold my body more erect and balance myself. Whoa, you have completely removed both of your hands from my hips and waist. I don't have complete control yet, so I'm going to let go of these toys and balance myself with both hands on the floor between my legs or next to my thighs. Oh, I like this; I'm doing it myself. I'm leaning forward and at times I must hold onto my feet, but I am doing it. I should have this perfected between four and seven months.

Sitting Unassisted

I released both hands and toppled over! It was a little scary, but since you didn't appear startled, I wasn't scared. I am so glad you provided this thick cushion. I will pull myself back into sitting position with a little help. Okay I'm back up now, with both hands on the floor next to my thighs.

What if I release one hand instead of both? Wow, I'm now sitting and supporting myself with one hand. I'm going to use this other hand to get that toy. I need to use the other hand that is supporting me to play with this toy. I'm going to let go. Wow! I'm sitting by myself and not toppling over. The room looks different from this position. Thanks. I've got it.

Crawling

I enjoy playing with my keys. They are way out of reach. I am on my tummy and reaching my right arm out so that I can grasp with my hand. Oh boy, this is not working. I'm going to try the other arm and hand. It's still not working. I'm going to try both at the same time. I still can't get them. If you were down here with me, I would whine so you could get them for me. I want those keys. Boy, do I want those keys!

Maybe, if I position my arms and hands just right, I can pull my body forward. Oh yeah, it worked—I moved a few inches. I still can't reach those keys. Maybe if I got on my knees and put my buttocks in the air I could do it. No, this isn't working because my hands and arms are in the way. Okay, I must think about this.

Maybe if I push all the way up on my arms and push my buttocks up in the air at the same time, it will work. Oh, wow! Oh, wow! I'm up! I'm now going to rock back and forth. Oh, wow, but I'm not moving. Uh oh, I am going to have to figure out how to coordinate moving my hands, arms, and knees at the same time. Okay, here we go. Uh oh! Topple, back up, move into position. Uh oh—topple, back up, move into position. Oh, me! Oh, my! I'm doing it! I'm doing it! Forget those keys; I'm going across the room. Oh, yeah! I am now 8 to 10 months and getting my "crawl" on.

Pulling to Stand and Cruising

I know these legs are made for more than just crawling. I see you using yours. I am now 6 to 10 months and wondering about this. I want to get up there onto the sofa with you. What? You're not going to pick me up? I'm going to pull on your leg and pull my body into standing position. I'm up. Whoa! You scooped me up, and you are showering me with these kisses while shouting, "You did it!" What did I do? I was only trying to get to you.

Okay, why is one of my favorite toys on one end of the sofa and one of my other favorite toys on the other end? I'm going to crawl over and check it out. I'm sitting here and looking up. I can't reach it from here. I'm going to get onto my knees. I still can't reach it. I'm going to pull my body into standing position. Oh, that's better—I got it.

I now want to play with that other toy on the other end of the sofa. If I hold on and take steps sideways—I can reach it. Sideways, step; sideways, step; sideways, step; sideways, step; sideways, step; sideways, step. Ooh, I'm getting my "cruise" on. Oh boy! Nine to 12 months! Oh, boy! I got it! I just *cruised* and got my other favorite toy.

Standing Independently

I am now 9 to 11 months old. This time is going fast. You are now on your knees, and I'm standing assisted with my back against your chest. What are you up to now? You are pushing me away from you, holding one of my hands, and pushing my feet so they are straight. You are now putting just your finger into my hand. As you feel me loosening my grip on your finger, you are gradually letting me go. Oh, me! Oh, my! I am standing all by myself—one second, two seconds, three seconds, four seconds … *plop*! Right down on my buttocks. I guess I'll sit here and think about this … hmmm.

Walking with Hands Held

Time is passing. It is now 10 to 13 months; you are standing behind me while holding both of my hands. We are walking all over this room. Okay, why are you moving to my side and letting my one hand go? Who is going to hold my other hand? I'm standing next to you, and you are starting to walk! Okay, I'm going to take steps with my one hand held. Oh boy, I'm falling again. Pull me up a little. I must push myself up to balance—I got it. I can now walk with one and both hands held without falling.

Walking by Myself

There you go kneeling behind me again. Oh my, what time is it? It is 11 to 14 months. Look who's in front of us a few feet away. He's calling me and holding out his arms. He's on his knees, too. If he wants me, I'm going to him. Okay, I'm going to push off you and stand by myself. I can do this. Without my hands held, I must balance my body on both sides.

Okay, here I go. Step, wobble, brace, pause. Step, wobble, brace, pause. Step, wobble, whoa, brace, pause. This takes a lot of concentration and coordination. Step, wobble, brace, pause. Step, wobble, brace. Step, wobble, brace. Step, wobble. Step, wobble. Step, step, step, step. I made it!

Whoa! He scoops me up and throws me into the air. You both are clapping and cheering so loudly. I squeal, cheer, and clap for myself. Let me walk behind my push toy. After a lot of practice, I now have walking mastered. I can now do a *hurried walk* and even run. Around 25 to 35 months, I will be jumping, kicking, throwing, catching, and walking up and down stairs. Engage me in these fun activities by modeling them for me. Hold both of my hands and let's jump together; place a stick on the floor and encourage me to jump over it. Show me how to kick by lifting one of my legs as you support my standing. Let me do it myself. Encourage my catching ability by extending both of my outstretched arms and holding them together. Move a few inches away and throw the ball. The ball will lodge into my arms. Teach me to walk up and down stairs by encouraging me to hold the rail with one hand and your hand with my other hand. Show me how to walk up and down steps. When I first start these actions at 18-24 months, there will be plenty of laughter as I learn. Let's have fun together. Thank you so much!

Development Assignment

Please review the following websites to learn more about my physical gross motor development. Please choose recommended strategies to add to your list of development activities. Review the milestones directly before my age, my age range, and beyond my age range. Example: If I am 12 months, review the milestones for 9-12, 12-15 and 15-18 months, so that you will know what to expect.

American Academy of Pediatrics website

Prenatal
https://www.healthychildren.org/English/ages-stages/prenatal/Pages/default.aspx

Baby
https://www.healthychildren.org/English/ages-stages/baby/Pages/default.aspx

Toddler
https://www.healthychildren.org/English/ages-stages/toddler/Pages/default.aspx

Preschool
https://www.healthychildren.org/English/ages-stages/
preschool/Pages/default.aspx

Gradeschool
https://www.healthychildren.org/English/ages-stages/
gradeschool/Pages/default.aspx

Developmental Milestones of Early Literacy
https://www.healthychildren.org/English/ages-stages/
baby/Pages/Developmental-Milestones-of-Early-Literacy.
aspx

What to Expect website

http://www.whattoexpect.com/milestones/

Zero to Three website

https://www.zerotothree.org/resources/series/your-child-
s-development-age-based-tips-from-birth-to-36-months

Physical Gross Motor Assessment

Name_____ Age_____

Skills

Tummy Time

First Attempt

How Often?

Concerns

Explores by Putting Things into Mouth

First Attempt

How Often?

Concerns

Head and Neck Control

First Attempt

How Often?

Concerns

Rolling Side to Back

First Attempt

How Often?

Concerns

Rolling from Back to Side

First Attempt

How Often?

Concerns

Rolling Stomach to Back

First Attempt

How Often?

Concerns

Rolling from Back to Stomach

First Attempt

How Often?

Concerns

Sitting Assisted

First Attempt

How Often?

Concerns

Sitting Unassisted

First Attempt

How Often?

Concerns

Crawling
First Attempt

How Often?

Concerns

Pulling to Stand

First Attempt

 How Often?

Concerns

Cruising

First Attempt

How Often?

Concerns

Standing All by Myself

First Attempt

How Often?

Concerns

Walking with Hands Held

First Attempt

How Often?

Concerns

Walking All by Myself

First Attempt

How Often?

Concerns

Jumping

First Attempt

How Often?

Concerns

Kicking

First Attempt

How Often?

Concerns

Throwing
First Attempt

How Often?

Concerns

Catching

First Attempt

How Often?

Concerns

Walking Up and Down Stairs

First Attempt

How Often?

Concerns

Questions for Pediatrician

Chapter 4

Physical Development— Let Me Move

Part 2: Fine Motor Development

Depending on how you engage me, all the fine motor skills discussed in this chapter should take place from 2 to 36 months.

Hands

My hands are tools that I will use for the rest of my life. Eventually, I will keep them open more often. As for now, kiss my balled-up little fists, and when I do have them open, kiss each finger. Engage me in play and watch me notice my hands as I move them about. I will put my hands into my mouth. I will wave my arms to touch the dangling toy overhead. Place a rattle in my hand and see how long I can hold it. I will not be able to hold it at first.

Over time, I will hold it for longer periods.

Place an object in my hands and I will put it into my mouth and chew on it. It may appear that I am eating the objects. I am not eating them; I am exploring them using my senses of taste, touch, and sight. If the object makes noise, I am also using my sense of hearing. The baby bath and shampoo used on my hair and skin has me smelling delightful; you smell good, too. Oh, there's the use of my sense of smell. We have all the senses covered.

I will eventually reach, grasp, drop, retain, bang, and transfer objects with each hand. At first, I will use both hands and eventually want to use one hand more than the other. I might even develop a preference for using both hands equally well. The term for this is *ambidextrous*. I am going to use my little hands to clap and wave bye-bye at twelve to fourteen months or before. Here's a great bye-bye song:

"See you later, alligator
After a while, crocodile
Bye-bye, butterfly
See you the next time."

Development Activities

Place your finger into the palm of my hand and watch me fold my hand around it. My grip will be very tight. Place me onto my back and allow me to play independently. I will grab my toes and feet with one hand and have the other hand in my mouth. I will release coos of incredible pleasure. I like my hands and feet. I like my feet so much that I will also begin to taste my toes.

Use hand-over-hand assistance to teach me to reach, grasp, drop, retain, bang, and transfer objects with each hand. Model the skills by playing with my toys as I watch. Place the toys near me to see if I can do the action. As you tell me bye-bye, lift my arm and hand up and down. Wave to me and say, "Bye-bye."

Pincer-Grasp

In the beginning, I will use my whole hand in a raking motion to pick up things. During the 7-month to 12-month range, please provide hand-over-hand assistance in which you place your hands over mine and engage me in the desired activity. This will teach me to use my *pincer-grasp* and enable me to hold an object between the tips of my thumb and index finger. Finger foods are a great way to teach this skill. Between 9 months and 24 months, I will be able to take small objects out of containers, put them into containers, release objects voluntarily, and stack blocks. I will be able to place many pegs into pegboards, and over time, make taller towers with my blocks.

Development Activities

Place finger foods and table food on my high chair tray or activity tray. Use hand-over-hand assistance and place the food between my thumb and index finger. Bring the food to my mouth. Repeat this activity and gradually lessen the assistance to see if I can do it independently. Eat the finger food yourself to model for me. Use many of my toys to engage me in this skill. Engage me in completing puzzles with and without knobs. Guide my hand to do this, and then allow me to do it independently.

As I hold a toy in one hand, encourage me to reach for another toy with my other hand. Give me pull-apart pop beads and watch me put them together and take them apart. Engage me in the shape sorter and watch me fit the shapes into their spaces. Stack blocks with me and encourage me to build tall towers. Laugh with delight as we knock them over.

Making Marks on Paper and Scribbling

In the beginning, I will hold pencils and crayons in a fisted hand. But as my pincer-grasp skill becomes more refined, I will be able to hold, in adult fashion, my crayons and any other writing tools. I will also be able to make marks on paper and then scribble. Please engage me. This is preparation for me to make my positive mark in the world. As this skill is more refined, I will be able to make vertical and horizontal strokes. I'll also be able to imitate circular scribble. The range for this will occur at eleven to thirty-six months.

Development Activities

Offer me many toys in a large container. Model removing them yourself and then offering them to me. Please engage me in toy play: putting on, taking off, putting in, and taking out. Encourage me to place certain colored pegs into the pegboard until the entire board is filled.

Place dry beans onto the table and encourage me to pick them up and place them into a container. This is a great way to introduce counting. Encourage me to count the beans with you. Place one bean on the table and say, "This is one bean." Now place another bean on the table and say, "Now we have two beans. Let's count them." Say, "One, two." Repeat and reinforce each time. I will eventually be able to count two objects without assistance.

Place an easel pad of paper onto the floor with my crayons and other writing tools. Sit me on the easel pad and let's engage in coloring. Offer me hand-over-hand assistance to hold the writing tools correctly. Make various shapes on the paper and encourage me to make them, too.

Other Tools

As my fine-motor development proceeds, give me some string and one-inch beads, and I will place the string through the beads all by myself. I've seen you use scissors.

Give me some child scissors and I will snip the paper with them. I will eventually be able to copy a circle and make my first designs and spontaneous forms. My fine motor skills must be developed, so try these around 20 months and continue through 36 months. I am so excited about these possibilities. Are you excited?

Development Activities

Place colored one-inch beads on the floor. Model picking up the beads and encourage me to do it. Encourage me to place the beads into a hole in the top of a box. Offer me other small objects to place into small containers. Tell me to watch you make vertical, horizontal, and circular strokes on the paper, and then encourage me to make my own strokes next to yours.

Give me play dough and other sculpting material. Encourage me to poke, pound, and build structures. Provide me with various containers with lids. Encourage me to screw off and screw on lids. Place things into containers for me to pour from one container to another.

Development Assignment

Please review the following websites to learn more about my physical fine motor development. Please choose recommended strategies to add to your list of development activities. Review the milestones directly before my age, my age range, and beyond my age range. Example: If I am 12 months, review the milestones for 9-12, 12-15 and 15-18 months, so that you will know what to expect.

American Academy of Pediatrics website

Prenatal
https://www.healthychildren.org/English/ages-stages/prenatal/Pages/default.aspx

Baby
https://www.healthychildren.org/English/ages-stages/
baby/Pages/default.aspx

Toddler
https://www.healthychildren.org/English/ages-stages/
toddler/Pages/default.aspx

Preschool
https://www.healthychildren.org/English/ages-stages/
preschool/Pages/default.aspx

Gradeschool
https://www.healthychildren.org/English/ages-stages/
gradeschool/Pages/default.aspx

Developmental Milestones of Early Literacy
https://www.healthychildren.org/English/ages-stages/
baby/Pages/Developmental-Milestones-of-Early-Literacy.
aspx

What to Expect website

http://www.whattoexpect.com/milestones/

Zero to Three website

https://www.zerotothree.org/resources/series/your-child-
s-development-age-based-tips-from-birth-to-36-months

Physical Fine Motor Assessment

Name_____ Age____

Skills

Uses Hands

First Attempt

How Often?

Concerns

Uses Pincer-Grasp
(Tip of Thumb and Index Finger)

First Attempt

How Often?

Concerns

Makes Marks on Paper

First Attempt

How Often?

Concerns

Scribbles

First Attempt

How Often?

Concerns

Use of Other Tools

First Attempt

How Often?

Concerns

Questions for Pediatrician

"Play is the highest expression of human development in childhood for it alone is the free expression of what is in a child's soul."

—Friedrich Frobel

Your Thoughts:

"Play is the work of childhood."

—Jean Piaget

Your Thoughts:

"In play, the child is always behaving beyond his age, above his usual everyday behavior; in play he is, as it were, a head above himself. Play contains in a concentrated form, as in the focus of a magnifying glass, all developmental tendencies; it is as if the child tries to jump above his usual level."

—Les Vygotsky

Your Thoughts:

"There is little that gives children greater pleasure than when a grown-up let's himself down to their level, renounces his oppressive superiority and plays with them as an equal."

—Sigmund Freud

Your Thoughts:

Chapter 5

Cognitive Development —Let Me Learn

Cognitive development is the ability to think and respond. *Cognition* depends on sensory input and perceptual processing. The study of this developmental domain centers on how young children come to understand the world they find themselves in, how they adapt to that world, and how they learn to represent it (Martin & Berke, 2007). Most of the information in this chapter will overlap the language, physical, social-emotional, and self-help development areas. This area of development is very extensive, so it is divided into four sections: reading, singing, thinking, and playing.

Reading

> "Read, read, read a book,
> Read one every day.
> Oh, I like it; oh, I like it.
> Include it in my play."

Thank you for reading to me while I was in the womb. Read to me on my first day of arrival into the world and every day thereafter. I'm sorry, maybe not the first day—I guess you'll be a little tired—ask any other family member to do it. I enjoy the closeness when you read to me. I enjoy the sound of your voice, your soft arms, and the way you smell. You sure know how to make the characters come alive. I like how you change your voice for the characters, and I like the animal sounds.

Show me the pictures, and provide hand-over-hand assistance for me to turn pages and point to the pictures as you say the object names. Eventually, between 12 and 36 months, I will be able to point to requested objects, name objects independently, make animal sounds, and recite ending phrases after you read the beginning of a sentence. Over time, and after many interactions with the same story, tell me to read to you. This is my *prereading stage*. Reading is an important foundation for my life, so read many books, daily, just for me at each age level. Don't miss a day. I am going to enjoy getting my "read" on. The guide below lists the different types of books that I like at different age ranges*:

INFANTS (6-12 months)

- Board books with photos of babies

- Sturdy, brightly colored board books to touch and taste

- Books with pictures of things I see every day: balls, bottles, chairs, dogs

- Small books sized for my small hands

YOUNGER TODDLERS (12-24 months)

- Sturdy board books I can handle and carry

- Books that show children doing familiar things: sleeping, eating, playing

- Good-night books for bedtime

- Books about saying good-bye and hello

- Books with only a few words on the page

- Books with simple rhymes or predictable text

OLDER TODDLERS (24-36 months)

- Books with pictures and names of many different things

- Books with board pages—but also books with paper pages

- Silly books and funny books

- Books with rhyme and rhythm and repeated text I can learn by heart

- Books about children and families

- Books about food, animals, trucks, and other of my favorite objects

*Taken from Reach Out and Read.org
https://www.reachoutandread.org/FileRepository/
WhatChildrenLikeinBooks.pdf

Development Activities

Read multiple stories to me daily. Cuddle me on your lap and hold the book so we can both see it. Change your voice to show happiness, sadness, or other feelings. Change your voice for each character. I may fall asleep in the first few months, but please finish the story. Over time, I will be wide awake and want you to read all the books. Take me to the public library; I am not too young. The staff is waiting for us and will provide a schedule for story hours. The librarian will also recommend popular titles that I will enjoy. Use the materials and book list in the resources section of this book to engage me in more literacy activities.

Provide stiff, hardbound books and soft-cover cloth books. Encourage me to help you turn the pages. While engaging me in my toys, stand books on the floor near my toys so that I will have a choice. Place books in baskets throughout the house—in the kitchen, bathroom, living room, den, and so on. Create a portable library with a decorative box that I can transport to any room.

Relate the stories to my personal experiences. Encourage me to talk about the characters and events in storybooks. Pause during your reading so I can recite entire phrases. Misread or leave words out of my favorite stories. Look for me to protest, please apologize, and then make the corrections. Also, ask me to make the corrections. Encourage me to read to you. Keep a record of all the books that I read. I will enjoy looking at the list when I am all grown up.

Singing

In a few months, I am going to begin to play with my hands, fingers, feet, and toes. Play "This Little Piggy Went to Market" with my toes: "This little piggy went to market, this little piggy stayed home …" You can do any variation. Tell me the names of my hands, fingers, feet, and toes, and I will know four body parts. Sing to me. I need to hear words sung to me. I need you to sing, "Twinkle, Twinkle, Little Star." "Twinkle, twinkle, little star"—open your hands and let your fingers touch your thumb rapidly to show the twinkle. Lift your hands up for, "Up above the world so high," and I will learn the preposition *up*. When you sing this song, the stars in my little world shine brighter. "The world so high"—the world does not seem like such a big, scary place when you are around. You are bigger and higher than everything in my world. I look up to you.

Sing me the "Barney Song" because I love you, you love me, we're a happy family. … Slow the song down and give me a hug. Slow the song down and shower me with many kisses. Slow it down and tell me how much you love me, too. I love you so much.

Let's sing the "*ABC* Song." I like that one. "*A, B, C, D …
LMNO …*" now I know my *ABCs*. At first, I will stare at you. I will then stare at you and smile. I will then stare, smile, and begin to rock my body to the rhythm. I will then make sounds and rock my body to the rhythm. I will then be able to sing certain letters and make sounds for others while rocking my body to the rhythm. Eventually, I will be able to sing the entire song. Make sure I can also say the letters in order as well as sing them. During the singing, I think *LMNOP* are one letter, so slow the song down and sing, "*L, M, N, O, P*." Thanks!

Please engage me in finger plays. I like the "Itsy-Bitsy Spider…climbed up the water spout." Pretend to make your fingers go up a web. Make your fingers come down like rain, and then push them out with force. Spread your arms up and wide for the sun. Use those fingers to dry the rain. Do the finger movements again! This is so much fun! Hold your hands over mine and show me how to do the movements. Let's do it again and again.

Do you know, "Where Is Thumbkin?" Do that one. This next one makes me so excited! I can barely get it out. "Head (deep breath), shoulders (giggles), knees, and toes"—let's do that one. Touch my head. Touch my shoulders. Touch my knees and toes. Touch my eyes, ears, mouth, and nose. I get so tickled when I touch the wrong body part, and when you speed up the song, I try to keep up. This one song will teach me eight body parts. You can keep the same tune and include other body parts that I will need to know. Eventually, I will know all my body parts.

Development Activities

Expose me to different kinds of music and encourage me to clap and bounce my body up and down to the music. Make sure you include classical music; it encourages my creativity. Give me rattles and blocks and model for me how to shake and bang them to the music. Engage me in making musical instruments: bells, drums, sticks, and rattles. Provide me with many musical toys with sounds, tunes, and songs. Encourage me to push the buttons to hear the sounds. Teach me how to whisper by increasing and decreasing the volume of your voice. Teach me how to hum. Teach me to dance and dance with me. Encourage me to initiate dancing and singing.

Thinking

Over time, I will be able to track you or any moving object with my eyes. At seven to nine months, I will also be able to find partially hidden objects. While I am watching, cover one of my toys with a cloth, and I will pull the cloth off to find it. I will begin to understand that even if it's hidden, it didn't go away; it still exists. This is referred to as *object permanence.*

Please teach me my name from day one by calling me by it. If you name me Charles, please don't call me Pookey all the time. If you name me Annie, don't call me Pooh-Pooh all the time. Make up a song that includes all the letters in my name, and I will eventually learn how to spell my name while singing the song. When I arrive at school, I will need to know and use my birth name.

Teach me whether I am a boy or a girl around 24 to 36 months or sooner. Say to me, "My name is (say your name) and I am a girl. Then ask, "What is your name? Wait for my response. Then ask, "Are you a boy or a girl?" You may have to tell me my name and sex. Repeat this procedure at various times and eventually I will tell you my name and my sex. Please identify all my friends with their names and sex; this will help me to learn faster.

Teach me, from birth until I learn them, all family member names as I interact with them. Refer to them even when they're not around. Over time, test me. While in the room with many family members, ask me where is ___ and insert his or her name. Watch me look directly at them. Over time, I will say their names. Teach me the gender of family members: boy, girl, woman, and man. If we have dogs or cats, teach me their names and the sounds they make. These will be my first animal sounds.

I will be able to respond to simple verbal requests. I will give you the ball, toy, or book when you ask. This will expand to include obeying two-part related and unrelated commands. Please ensure that I can follow one simple verbal request before you engage me in two-part related and unrelated commands. Ask me to "Get the toy and put it in the toy box," or "Pick up the cup and put it on the table." Don't overload me and frustrate yourself; make sure I understand. Oh, by the way, at nine to twelve months, make sure I understand "no-no" and stop whatever action I'm doing. At this age, I will still act like I don't understand "no-no" because I do not want to stop.

Look for signs that I understand "no-no." I might pull to stand next to the table and be tempted to touch the lamp that you told me not to touch. I want to touch that lamp. Boy, do I want to touch that lamp! I look at it intently, and then look at you. You are staring at me, not smiling, and have folded your arms. You are not saying any words. I know what intense eye contact, body posture, and silence means. I will then look back at the lamp, stare at it intensely, not touch it, and say "no-no," as if the lamp is touching me. I saved that lamp from getting into trouble! I will then get down and go play with my toys. You can laugh internally, but do not laugh out loud. I am processing at my level, and if you laugh, I will think it is a joke and turn it into a game.

Please don't get frustrated with me because at thirteen months, as I develop more independence, "no" will be one of my favorite and most highly used words, possibly before I understand what "no-no" means. I will even sometimes say "no" when I mean "yes." You might want to use some other terms to stop my undesirable actions. "No-no" has already been claimed by me and many other two-year-olds. Whatever term you use, make sure you use it consistently and that I understand what it means.

Development Activities

While singing and talking to me, ensure that I am showing interest by looking at you, responding, and engaging. Stand on the other side of the room out of my vision range. Begin to talk and make sure that I turn to look in your direction. If I don't readily look, come closer and do it again.

Place toys and books in various sections of the floor as I watch. Include items for pretend and imaginative play. Tell me to wait until you have everything set up. Announce that you are ready. Follow me to whatever toys I choose and engage me. When I decide to play with another toy, follow me there and engage me. Follow my lead. Match the toys that you arrange to my developmental level.

Playing

Please play peek-a-boo at six months or before and watch me smile or laugh hysterically. Once I have full use of my arms, hands, and fingers, I am going to enjoy throwing. This will last a long time—9 to 12 months and beyond. Remember my potential; I might be preparing for a sports career. I will throw everything. Please provide soft toys and balls that I can throw instead of stopping me from engaging in such wonderful play. Of course, set those limits because I will also enjoy throwing my cup, plate, spoon, and food to the floor as I sit in my high chair. I know this is not appropriate, but I do enjoy it.

At 10 months, watch me take these rings off this stacker. Look at all the colors. The object at this stage is not for me to put them back on or in order; this will come over time around 30 to 36 months or before, so don't stress me. Provide me with many toys so I can match shapes and colors. Eventually, I will sort shapes and complete multiple-piece puzzles. Engage me in cause and effect with many mechanical toys that make noise or do something. Engage me, at 18 to 24 months, in play dough, paint, sand, water, letters, and numbers. Provide preplanned learning opportunities to work on developmental skills that I have yet to master. *Preplanned learning opportunities* are activities that you organize with my toys to engage me in specific skills. Constantly assess or evaluate my developing skills. As I master developmental skills, please move me on to more difficult skills.

Engage me in clean-up time with my toys. Start this at 12 months or before. It is recommended at 21 months. Make it fun, be creative. Sing the "Clean-Up Song": "Clean up, clean up, everybody everywhere, clean up, clean up, everybody do your share." Extend my clean-up ability into the following routines: breakfast, snack, lunch, dinner, putting clothes away, and so on. Teach me that there is a place for everything, and everything needs to be in its place. The mastery of this skill will provide me with a more disciplined life now and in the future. Again, play is my work and my work is play. This is how I learn.

Development Activities

Engage me in dress-up play with male and female clothing. Let me use your old clothes, hats, and bags. Make sure the clothing is easy to put on and take off. Engage me in play with other children. In the beginning, I will play next to them without much interaction with them and more interaction with the toys. This is called *parallel play*. Over time, I will imitate the play of another child and play simple interactive games. Use the play with other children to assess my developing skills. Do not make comparisons and worry that I lag far behind or that I'm a genius. Development is contingent upon a child's individual timetable and level of engagement experiences.

Development Assignment

Please review the following websites to learn more about my cognitive development. Please choose recommended strategies to add to your list of development activities. Review the milestones directly before my age, my age range, and beyond my age range. Example: If I am 12 months, review the milestones for 9-12, 12-15 and 15-18 months, so that you will know what to expect.

America Academy of Pediatrics website

Prenatal
https://www.healthychildren.org/English/ages-stages/
prenatal/Pages/default.aspx

Baby
https://www.healthychildren.org/English/ages-stages/
baby/Pages/default.aspx

Toddler
https://www.healthychildren.org/English/ages-stages/
toddler/Pages/default.aspx

Preschool
https://www.healthychildren.org/English/ages-stages/
preschool/Pages/default.aspx

Gradeschool
https://www.healthychildren.org/English/ages-stages/
gradeschool/Pages/default.aspx

Developmental Milestones of Early Literacy
https://www.healthychildren.org/English/ages-stages/
baby/Pages/Developmental-Milestones-of-Early-Literacy.
aspx

What to Expect website

http://www.whattoexpect.com/milestones/

Zero to Three website

https://www.zerotothree.org/resources/series/your-child-
s-development-age-based-tips-from-birth-to-36-months

Cognitive Assessment—Reading

Name_____ Age_____

Skills

Enjoys Listening to Stories

First Attempt

How Often?

Concerns

Looks at Pictures

First Attempt

How Often

Concerns

Hand-over-Hand Assistance to Points to Objects in Books

First Attempt

How Often?

Concerns

Enjoys Trips to the Library

First Attempt

How Often?

Concerns

Cognitive Assessment—Singing

Name_____ Age____

Skills

Enjoys "This Little Piggy"

First Attempt

How Often?

Concerns

Enjoys "Twinkle, Twinkle Little Star"

First Attempt

How Often?

Concerns

Enjoys "Barney Song"

First Attempt

How Often?

Concerns

Enjoys the "*ABC* Song"

First Attempt

How Often?

Concerns

Sings Some Letters from "*ABC* Song"

First Attempt

How Often?

Concerns

Sings All Letters from "*ABC* Song"

First Attempt

How Often?

Concerns

Can Say Alphabet in Order

First Attempt

How Often?

Concerns

Enjoys "Itsy, Bitsy Spider"

First Attempt

How Often?

Concerns

Enjoys the Music and Movement to the Song "Head, Shoulders, Knees, and Toes"

First Attempt

How Often?

Concerns

Touches Some Body Parts during Song "Head, Shoulders, Knees, and Toes"

First Attempt

How Often?

Concerns

Touches Head, Shoulders, Knees, and Toes during the Song

First Attempt

How Often?

Concerns

Questions for Pediatrician

Cognitive Assessment—Thinking

Name_____ Age____

Skills

Finds Partially Hidden Object

First Attempt

How Often?

Concerns

Knows Name

First Attempt

How Often?

Concerns

Knows Own Gender

First Attempt

How Often?

Concerns

Knows Family Names

First Attempt

How Often?

Concerns

Can Say Family Names

First Attempt

How Often?

Concerns

Responds to Simple Verbal Requests

First Attempt

How Often?

Concerns

Obeys Two-Part Related Commands

First Attempt

How Often?

Concerns

Obeys Two-Part Unrelated Commands

First Attempt

How Often?

Concerns

Understands "No-No" and Stops Action

First Attempt

How Often?

Concerns

"No" Highly Used Word

First Attempt

How Often?

Concerns

Obeys Two-Part Related Commands

First Attempt

How Often?

Concerns

Obeys Two-Part Unrelated Commands

First Attempt

How Often?

Concerns

Questions for Pediatrician

Cognitive Assessment—Playing

Name_____ Age____

Skills

Enjoys Peek-a-Boo

First Attempt

How Often?

Concerns

Plays Peek-a-Boo

First Attempt

How Often?

Concerns

Enjoys Throwing

First Attempt

How Often?

Concerns

Takes Rings off Stacker

First Attempt

How Often?

Concerns

Puts Rings on Stacker, No Order

First Attempt

How Often?

Concerns

Puts Rings on Stacker in Order

First Attempt

How Often?

Concerns

Sings "Clean-Up Song"

First Attempt

How Often?

Concerns

Participates in Clean-Up

First Attempt

How Often?

Concerns

Questions for Pediatrician

"When we are polite to children, we show in the most simple and direct way possible that we value them as people and care about their feelings."

—David Elkind

Your Thoughts:

Social-Emotional Development—Let Me Feel

Social-emotional development concerns the infant or young child's identity, relationships with others, and understanding of his or her place within the social environment. *Personality development* considers the temperament types of children and how they remain surprisingly constant throughout life (Martin & Berke, 2007). (See chapter 1.)

Stimulation

At the beginning of my life, I will enjoy and need a great deal of physical contact and tactile stimulation in which I relate to your sense of touch. It is very important that I establish eye contact from the beginning. I need to draw attention to myself when I'm in distress and respond with a smile when people talk to me. I will become quiet to a familiar face or voice. Again, I need to get my "coo" and "babble" on in response to adult talk and smiles.

Development Activities

Gently stroke my fingers, hands, toes, arms, legs, and feet with your fingertips. Ooh, your soft touch feels so good. Name the body parts as you touch them and tell me how special I am and how much you love me. Human touch is healing, soothing, and powerful. Touch stimulates my physical growth and brain development.

Reciprocal Interactions

Our interactions need to be shared and felt by both of us. There needs to be a shared emotional exchange between us. I need to recognize you and begin to lift my arms when you want to hold me. I also need to begin to lift them when I want to be held by you. I am going to begin to move away from you and show anxiety, fear, or nervousness when being separated from you. This is called *separation anxiety*.

This independence journey is very confusing to me. I have been so attached to you. Why does it have to end? Oh, but I do want it to end. With all of this occurring at 5 to 10 months, am I ready to be separate from you?

Development Activities

Play peek-a-boo and pat-a-cake with me often; watch my response and level of engagement. Engage me in play with adults so that I can begin to imitate the actions of adults: play dress-up with male and female clothing, clean the house, go shopping, and take care of a baby. Engage me in play with other children so I can become aware of the feelings displayed by others. I may begin to show empathy by crying when I hear or see another child cry. I may repeat an action that makes an adult laugh or smile.

Continue to engage me in play with other children so that I can use my words to play or respond to another child who wants to play. Engage me in activity and tell me when another child is sad or hurt. I will begin to eventually respond to other children's feelings by patting their backs or kissing their boo-boos. I will also show interest in a preferred playmate.

Independent Behavior

I need you to fully prepare yourself for the next part of this journey from 9 to 12 months. I am going to test your reactions during feeding (do I want this to eat, or do I want that?) and bedtime (I'm not ready to go; I want to play; I need a snack). When I turn 12 months, you are going to know it, and the whole world will know it. I'm either walking or about to walk. When I stand tall, the world looks different. I must conquer it. My self-reliant behavior is going to surface. I will feel that I don't need you and can do everything all by myself. I may be difficult to discipline and enter the "no" stage. I may act impulsively, doing things suddenly and without careful thought. I may have a difficult time following rules.

Development Activities

Be aware of what frightens me or makes me anxious. Acknowledge these feelings and don't make me feel that they are not important. Watch my responses that indicate how I feel. Discuss my emotions with me. Discuss your emotions with me.

Offer me choices to determine my likes and dislikes. Acknowledge how I get upset when things don't go my way. Be firm and determine which things need to be addressed and which need to be ignored. Monitor what occurs before, during, and after situations that upset me. Especially take note of whether I can regulate my emotions and return to a happy state after being upset. Also, take note of how long it takes for me to regulate my behavior. Use the components of the time before, during, and after upsetting situations as teachable moments to help me guide my behavior.

The "No" Stage

Hold on—don't leave me at 12 to 18 months. I will attempt to direct myself and will resist any help doing it. Because I know you are in charge and I'm competing for the position, I will have frequent tantrums, and they will escalate. This is part of my development. I will need you to purposefully guide my behavior as I don't have enough experience to guide it myself.

Development Activities

Engage me in activities that will assist my growing sense of being separate from you. Engage me in activities that develop my emerging skills and independence. Highlight the behaviors that hurt me or others. Be firm but loving. Bring your emotional level down to zero as you engage in my heightened emotional levels. Deal with me with logic and you will help me gain a sense of mastery and achievement. Create a delicate balance of celebrating me and correcting me.

Resistance

Are you still holding on? By the age of 12 to 24 months (oh, no; this overlaps the "no" stage), I will feel that the world revolves around me and be jealous of any attention that is not directed at me. My emotions will be so unpredictably happy one minute, sad the next. I will get frustrated and mad over what seems unimportant to you. I will show a variety of emotions, sometimes at the same time—I will sympathize with you and then show anger. I'll be brave and then fearful. I will be proud and then show modesty.

These emotions will hit me all at once and make me want to fight and resist if you try to comfort me. I will then show you an incredible amount of love after this wave of emotion subsides. This will make me frustrated and teary. Because I don't have control of my many emotions, an easy response will be a temper tantrum, during which I will resist and fight. This will cause even more frustration. I love you. I don't want to resist and fight you, but I must. I will be demanding and appear to be in charge.

These characteristics are part of this stage of my development. Don't be discouraged. Don't take it personally. The behaviors might be terrible, but I'm still terrific. Please don't call me a baby anymore. When I hear this, it makes me upset. I am not a baby! I am big now! I will try to imitate the activities that you do, such as cleaning the house and shopping. Listen for my words, "I can do it" and "Let me do it." The use of these words is a healthy sign of independence. The way you handle this stage will dictate my behavior in adulthood. You don't want me to display impulsive characteristics in adulthood. Don't give up! Read the last chapter, "Guiding Behavior," to implement strategies that will help us through this necessary but challenging developmental stage.

Development Activities

Allow me to explore the environment and find out who I am and what I can do. Provide me with many opportunities to engage in what I can do. Teach me how to ask for help with the things that are challenging for me. Offer me choices. These options must be appropriate so that whichever one I choose will increase my independence. Don't offer choices that are inappropriate and that will cause you stress in your ability to deliver.

Development Assignment

Please review the following websites and to learn more about my social-emotional development. Please choose recommended strategies to add to your list of development activities. Review the milestones directly before my age, my age range, and beyond my age range. Example: If I am 12 months, review the milestones for 9-12, 12-15 and 15-18 months, so that you will know what to expect.

American Academy of Pediatrics website

Prenatal
https://www.healthychildren.org/English/ages-stages/prenatal/Pages/default.aspx

Baby
https://www.healthychildren.org/English/ages-stages/baby/Pages/default.aspx

Toddler
https://www.healthychildren.org/English/ages-stages/toddler/Pages/default.aspx

Preschool
https://www.healthychildren.org/English/ages-stages/preschool/Pages/default.aspx

Gradeschool
https://www.healthychildren.org/English/ages-stages/gradeschool/Pages/default.aspx

Developmental Milestones of Early Literacy
https://www.healthychildren.org/English/ages-stages/baby/Pages/Developmental-Milestones-of-Early-Literacy.aspx

What to Expect website

http://www.whattoexpect.com/milestones/

Zero to Three website

https://www.zerotothree.org/resources/series/your-child-s-development-age-based-tips-from-birth-to-36-months

Social-Emotional Assessment

Name_____ Age____

Skills

Enjoys Physical Contact

First Attempt

How Often?

Concerns

Enjoys Tactile Stimulation

First Attempt

How Often?

Concerns

Enjoys Reciprocal Interactions

First Attempt

How Often?

Concerns

Experiences Separation Anxiety

First Attempt

How Often?

Concerns

Displays Independent Behavior

First Attempt

How Often?

Concerns

Has Difficulty in Guiding Behavior

First Attempt

How Often?

Concerns

Enters the "No" Stage

First Attempt

How Often?

Concerns

Resists Adult Control

First Attempt

How Often?

Concerns

Questions for Pediatrician

"The essence of independence is to be able to do something for one's self. Adults work to finish a task, but the child works in order to grow, and is working to create the adult, the person that is to be. Such experience is not just play ... it is work he must do in order to grow up."

—Maria Montessori

Your Thoughts:

"What a child can do today with assistance, she will be able to do by herself tomorrow."

—Lev Vygotsky

Your Thoughts:

Chapter 7

Self-Help Development— "Let Me Do It"

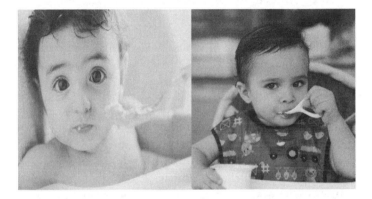

The more you do for me, the less I will do for myself. Please help me to help myself. I am helpless and unable to do many things that I will do later. Please don't leave me in this stage. Help me and enable me.

Self-help skills are skills that demonstrate the ability to eat, dress, keep clean, or toilet by oneself (Martin & Berke, 2007). Routines are a critical part of this developmental stage. Please provide a routine for the following times: wake-up, breakfast, snack, lunch, nap, diapering, dressing, playing, learning, cleaning-up, hand washing, dinner, bath time, bedtime, and so on. Provide age-appropriate routines from birth to three years old and beyond.

Here is an example of a wake-up routine: be excited to see me when I wake up in the morning; sing a "good morning" song to me; hug and kiss me; ask me how I slept; tell me how you slept; tell me what day it is; tell me what time it is; tell me what we are going to do throughout the day; tell me which routine comes next. Here is an example of a snack routine: announce that it is almost time for a snack; offer five-, three-, and two-minute warnings; wash my hands; dry my hands; sit me at the table; offer me a choice of two snacks; allow me to help with the preparation; eat the snack; clean-up; wash my hands; then tell me which routine comes next.

Teach me the parts of each routine so I will know what to expect. Inform me of the beginning of the routine, and please have a fancy ending for each. Some examples you can use for endings are: "ta-da," "all done," "you're nice and clean now," and so on. I will begin to assist you during each routine as early as four months depending on the routine. Look for signs of my participation. Allow enough time for the routines so that you do not rush yourself or me and miss the ways that I try to assist you. Give us time.

Please have a bedtime for me that you and I both recognize. Please don't let me go to bed whenever I want, when I get tired, or when you go. I am not an adult and need the limits set. Here is a possible routine for bedtime: announce that it is almost bedtime; give a five-minute warning, three-minute warning, two-minute warning; snack; story; hug; get into bed. As much as possible, put me to bed at the same time every night. If you do the same thing, the same way, at the same time for every routine, there will be less, if any, resistance from me. I will become more responsible because I am part of something important.

Co-sleeping

My journey of independence starts on the first day of my life. Bassinets, cribs, and baby monitors were made for a reason—to ensure that I sleep by myself. Please put me in my bassinet or crib from day one. Place me in the pediatric-recommended sleeping position, on my back. It is dangerous to allow me to sleep with you, other family members, or caregivers. You could roll over on me and crush me, or I could suffocate in the sheets and blankets.

Even though you know the dangers, it is still going to be tempting for you to do it. Some nights, you are going to be very tired because I will need to be fed in the middle of the night. Eventually, I will sleep through the night. It will seem easier to feed me in your bed and allow me to sleep there. It's not easier. I will get used to the warmth of your body and your smell. I will then never want to sleep in my crib alone and will scream if you place me there.

One day, you will look up, and I will be two or three years old and still sleeping in your bed. There are some adult tendencies I will take on at this stage. There are also some things that happen in your bed that I do not need to be aware of. Because your bed is a position of power, I will feel more in charge when engaging with you. I will feel like your equal. If you start putting me to sleep in your bed, it will be hard to stop, so please don't start.

Breastfeeding

Your breast is a very important tool. I recognize its importance from the first moment I use it. That "liquid gold" is amazing. I am making the connection to you. You are beautiful. After a few encounters, I want that breast milk. I need it. I've got to have it. Please give it to me. You and that breast meet my nourishment needs. It is designed just for me. The breast milk transforms itself to meet my needs at every feeding and throughout every stage. If I'm hungry when anyone else is holding me, male or female, I will check to see if they have any milk in their breast for me. If they don't, I will reject them immediately, cry, and look for you.

Watch what you eat, because it will be passed on to me. This will come in handy now and later when I transition to baby food. You are going to need to determine when to stop breastfeeding me. I will never want to stop if you leave it up to me. I can breastfeed for years! Talk to your doctor and others who successfully transitioned their children from breastfeeding. I can imagine that this will be hard for you and me. Remember, your goal is to make me independent.

Bottle Feeding

The bottle is also a very important tool. I recognize its importance from the first moment I use it. It is challenging to suck, swallow, and breathe with this bottle. I like how you hold it for me. I need both arms and hands to begin holding it as early as four months. Take that arm and hand that is positioned ever so comfortably around your waist and bring them out so they are aligned with my other hand and arm.

Please don't jab the bottle into my mouth. If I haven't begun to cry when I'm hungry by the time I'm three months old, hold the bottle in front of me and tell me, "Here's your bottle." Watch my anticipation. My arms will flail in various directions; my legs will kick, and my mouth will begin to pucker and those coos will emerge. Provide hand-over-hand assistance and guide my arms and hands to reach for my bottle.

Provide continued hand-over-hand assistance for me to hold the bottle for the entire feeding. If I release my hands from under your hand, stop the feeding so that I will connect that if I'm not holding the bottle with you, feeding will cease. Don't get into a battle with me. If I absolutely refuse to hold it, I may not be ready to engage with you. If I have already begun to cry, please don't take me through this process again because I am already agitated and will not learn. Please just give me my bottle. If you change the size of the bottle because I begin to drink more, you might have to start the process all over again because the bottle will be heavier and will not fit into my little hands. Over time, I will hold my bottle all by myself and will not need assistance. I will do it!

Baby Food

This breastfeeding or bottle is not enough. I need more. It's time to transition to baby food. Please decrease my breast milk or formula intake and increase my baby food. If you continue with the same amount of breast milk or formula, I will think baby food is optional and eventually will not want it. It is not optional. That is why baby food comes in stages. They make stage one for four-month-olds and refer to them as "supported sitters." Stage two is for six-month-olds, and they refer to them as "sitters." Finally, stage three is for eight-month-olds, and they refer to them as "crawlers." Show me the spoon as you feed me. This process will soon come in handy.

Table Food

Baby food will no longer be enough, and you will then need to transition me to table food. Stage three ends at eight months. Please let me eat at the table while others are eating. I will eat more. Prepare a plate for me, a small portion, and don't allow me to eat from your plate. This is a way to track how much I'm eating. Remember, my stomach is only the size of my clenched fist. I will start out eating with my hands—allow me to do this so I can understand the concept of eating and enjoy my food. The mess may make you uneasy. This is a stage on the way to independence. Keep the goal of the spoon in your mind as I learn to eat with my hands. As I eat with my hands, I'm watching you use your utensils to eat your food.

I will need to tolerate a wider variety of foods. I will need to safely chew and swallow a variety of textured foods. You will need to cook healthy food for me to develop a taste for it. If you offer me junk food and fast food during this time, you will be challenged. My taste buds will always prefer junk and fast food over healthy food. If you don't introduce junk and fast food, I won't know that they exist. Please, around eight to nine months and beyond, help me to get my "healthy food" on.

The Spoon

Oh, that wonderful spoon—time to use it with your assistance and then all by myself around nine to eighteen months! Sit behind me and offer hand-over-hand assistance as we both hold my spoon together. If you are behind me, you will match the exact direction I need to use it. If you do hand-over-hand in front of me, I will be learning two directions when I only need to learn one. The direction is optional; I am going to learn to use it no matter which angle you choose to teach me. Learning to use my spoon is easiest when you offer me oatmeal, yogurt, and applesauce as these adhere to the spoon.

Scoop, raise, angle into mouth; scoop, raise, angle into mouth; scoop, raise, angle into mouth. Ease your hand off a little and watch me scoop. Put your hand back over mine and help me raise and angle the spoon into my mouth. Ease your hand off a little while I scoop again. This time, ease your hand off a little while I raise and angle the spoon into my mouth. This is very difficult as I must coordinate my hand and my wrist to keep the spoon from turning over in the opposite direction. Look, I'm doing it myself!

Don't ever let me play with the spoon. It is a tool, not a toy. Stay with me through many meals, and do this process each time. Eventually, I will push away from you and say, "I do it." Watch me do it, and if I need any assistance, provide it. I will also master the use of the fork. I should have these mastered by thirty months or before.

Transition from Bottle to Cup

Hi, it's me again. I am now ready to transition from this bottle to a sippy cup somewhere between six to eighteen months. It's such a wide range because you and I both like the bottle. You must give me a sippy cup and explain to me what to do with it. If I just stare at it, provide hand-over-hand assistance—stand behind my chair, and place each of my hands onto the cup with your hands over mine. Bring the cup to my mouth. If I drink from it, I'm ready.

The offer of the sippy cup is to replace the bottle and take me to the next level. Please don't offer me the sippy cup and the bottle. If I have a choice, I will choose the bottle because I am accustomed to using it.

Please explain to me that my bottles are going bye-bye, and if you want to, have a ceremony in which I place all my bottles into a bag and we take them bye-bye. After you allow me to place every bottle in the house into a bag, we can take them to the garbage can at the curb, throw it in, and then wait for the garbage truck to come. Let me watch them put my bottles into that big truck. You know I like to watch that truck. When my bottles go into that truck, I will know there are no more bottles in the house.

Bye-bye, bottles! Don't save one in the cabinet for "just in case" because you will be tempted to give it to me if I cry and say "ba-ba" later that evening. This ritual is just as much for you as it is for me. If you don't do it this way, you will be telling all your friends that I just don't like any sippy cup that you have purchased. That's not true; I'm ready when you are. I might not ever cry for the bottle after this transition, or I might cry hysterically later that afternoon.

If I do cry because of being separated from my bottle, the cry will be very intense and last for hours with my saying "ba-ba" over and over. I will walk around in circles and go from room to room. I will look at you with a sadness that you have never seen before. I will reject the cup every time it is offered. You must remain strong and realize that you are taking me on the road to independence.

Offer me the cup. If I cry and reject it, take it back so I do not have the opportunity to throw it. Remain firm and tell me no more bottles. Do this no more than three times. Do not say anything after the third time or offer me the cup again. Do not take a trip to Walmart to get me another bottle. If you do, you will have to start this process all over again.

Offer me minimal comfort; this is something that I am going to have to work through. I might take the cup that night or the next day. I will take the cup because I want my milk, water, or juice. If this is the only way to get it, I will give in. The acceptance and use of my cup after the twenty-four-hour-or-less period of my crying hysterically is going to shock you. You are going to feel more confident in taking me to other levels of independence. I am going to have more confidence in your parenting skills and develop more trust and love for you. Remember, you are in charge, not me.

The goal is to transition from the sippy cup to the open cup by twenty-four months or before. Please use the little plastic cups that I see you rinse your mouth with in the bathroom. These are the perfect size to help me to learn to drink from the open cup. I will learn to control how much tilt to use to get the liquid into my mouth without spilling. A larger cup will be challenging because I will not know how much tilt to use, and the liquid will come out of my mouth, spill onto my clothes, and frustrate you and me. After I have mastered this, you can use a larger cup.

Potty Training and Diapering

Potty training begins at birth. It starts with the very first diaper change. Diapers were invented to make life easier for you and me. Please monitor my intake and my output—there's a connection. Monitor the time that I urinate or do a bowel movement. The monitoring will come in handy now and when you transition me to use the toilet.

It is crucial that you change me immediately after I wet or soil my diaper. I will assist you with this through crying because I don't like the feel against my skin. This is the beginning of my informing you that I have wet or soiled my diaper. Don't ignore this; it is important now and will be very important later. Please explain the process of the diaper change as you do it.

If I'm a girl, there are no surprises. If I'm a boy, take cover. (I really do mean to take cover.) It is something about my diaper being removed and that wonderful cool air hitting me that makes me want to squirt urine everywhere. If this is your first time diapering me, you are going to be shocked. You are going to squeal and whimper. You will move around in circles and not know how to stop the flow. I guess you'll be prepared to cover me with a towel the next time. Please don't use the new diaper to cover me, because I will wet a brand-new diaper that you will then discard. The first time is always a charm!

Speak and sing to me. This is a great bonding opportunity. Tell me how special I am and how much you love me. Please give me names for these processes of elimination. Urination and bowel movement are the proper names for these processes. Feel free to use these or your own names. Again, please don't use the bad word for the bowel movement, because I will use it.

As my development proceeds, I will eventually be able to assist you in diaper changes by getting the diaper and the wipes at nine months or before if you teach me. I will also be able to assist by lifting my legs and remaining still to make it easier. Please develop a set of steps for this routine, and do it the same way every time. Give me a toy or another object to hold while changing me. This will help me to avoid turning it into playtime where I try to flip and turn as you try to get the diaper off or put it on me. They have made diapers super absorbent now, and this allows me to stay drier through elimination. Continue to stick to the schedule and remove the diaper immediately. Thanks!

Potty-Training Readiness

I'm now old enough to inform you that I have wet or soiled my diaper by tapping it, pulling it, naming the process, and coming near you twelve to eighteen months or before if you teach me. I told you the monitoring of my intake, elimination, and changing me immediately would pay off. This is a big step. Please take note of it, and tell me how great I am for letting you know. That feeling of pride that I get from you saying this will encourage me to continue to tell you.

At this juncture, transition the diaper-changing conversation into potty-training preparation. Tell me about the potty or the toilet. You can use a training seat on the toilet or a potty chair on the floor. Either method is going to get me trained. These conversations are making me very excited because I see you use the big toilet. Thank you for making me part of the process and telling me what to expect. I am enjoying reading the "potty book" with you, and I know if that child, kitty, and doggy in the book can do it, I can do it.

Potty-Training Preparation

Thank you for clapping after I sat on the toilet for one minute while you supervised at 18 months or before. Don't stress yourself if this extends to 24 months or beyond. I didn't even cry. I didn't do anything, but I didn't cry. You are sitting with me again as I sit on the toilet. Uh, oh! Tinkle, tinkle, toot, I did it! Remember, potty train me when I can control my bladder and bowel functions.

What? Where are we going? We are going to get my new potty seat or potty chair and underwear. Wow! I feel so big now. I can get my potty seat or chair and underwear with pictures of my favorite characters. Thanks. What? I can even get an Elmo watch to wear on my arm? I won't have accidents because Elmo will alarm me when I need to go. I love Elmo! The watch is optional. Even without that watch, I'm not going to have accidents because I don't want to soil my favorite characters on my underwear. I'm so big now, and I can do it. Yes, I will let you know every time before I need to use the potty.

What? When we get home, we can't use them immediately. But why not? Because you want to give me a week to further prepare. Okay, I can't wait. Will you tell me how many days I have? I'm going to call everyone to tell them I have my new potty seat for the big toilet and my new underwear. What day do I need to tell them I will get started? Okay, next Tuesday.

Thanks for getting me underwear. I'm not going to have accidents in my underwear. No way, not my new underwear! When I first begin potty training, you can continue to use a diaper or pull-up on me at night to avoid accidents. Immediately when I awaken, ensure that I use the potty, and if my diaper, pull-up, or underwear is dry—celebrate this. Tell me how big I am! Please limit my liquid intake two hours before bedtime, and remember to let me go to the toilet before bedtime to help avoid accidents.

Development Activities

As a boy, I will need to master both sitting and standing. When I first start, just let me sit so that I can master how to do it. Over time, I am going to want to stand like all the men in my life. When I begin standing, teach me the process of aiming. If this is not taught, I might think that I have a water hose in my hands and need to water the toilet seat, walls, and floor.

Place a few bits of toilet tissue into the toilet and encourage me to aim at it. You can also try cheerios and froot loops to teach me to aim. If you use froot loops you can also teach me to aim at a specific color. Teach me how to place my penis downward into the toilet. This will help to guide the process. After I urinate, I will need to shake my penis for it to dry.

Teach me to focus, because if I talk to you as I do it, I will turn to face you and OOPS! Be patient with me. Remember to teach me to put the toilet seat up to use it and down when finished. Remind me to put it all the way up. OUCH! YOU FORGOT! That seat fell down on my penis! I will remember the next time, even if you forget to remind me. Teach me to flush and wash my hands. When I have it mastered, I will allow myself enough time if I need to stand to urinate or sit for a bowel movement.

As a girl, I will need to master sitting only. Teach me to pat dry. After I master potty training, teach me to wipe from front to back. Whether I am a boy or a girl, lavish on the praise during the process!

Assisted and Independent Dressing

Please make bathing and diapering as pleasant and enjoyable as possible. I will begin to smile or laugh in anticipation of these routines. Here is a bath-time routine: announce that it is almost bath time; five-minute warning, three-minute warning, two-minute warning; get towel; get pajamas; get bath toys; place bath toys into tub; play with bath toys for five minutes supervised; wash up; take bath toys out of tub; dry off; put on pajamas; hug; and then tell me which routine comes next. These are great routines in which to continue to teach me body parts. These successful experiences will help me when it's time for dressing all by myself.

Please remember to clean my teeth the moment that first tooth appears. Wipe my mouth with a damp cloth, touching my first teeth and tongue. Over time, begin to use a child-size, soft toothbrush. Allow me to watch you brush your teeth. Add a song and make sure it is part of my daily grooming routine. Ask the dentist for more strategies. Eventually, I will brush my teeth all by myself.

Please gently move my body parts into the desired clothing and tell me the body part you are moving from birth through the time that I can dress independently. Over time, watch for the slightest movement of body parts as you dress me. As time progresses, tell me to lift my precious little arms or legs. Prepare me as you place anything over my head. If you don't tell me, it will take my breath away, and the next time I will fight you so that you can't put that shirt over my head. As you engage me in grooming, watch me identify myself in the mirror at 14 to 16 months. Oh, that's you in the mirror with me. That mirror can be used to help me see myself do many things such as singing, reading, identifying body parts, and so on. Be creative and use my own reflection to teach me more skills. Please provide extra time for dressing and undressing. Eventually, at around 15 months, I will be able to take off my shoes, socks, pants, shirt, and underwear.

Please provide me enough time to do this without rushing me. Please celebrate this. Over more time, by 24 to 32 months, I will be able to put on my socks, pants, shirt, underwear, and shoes by myself. Carefully assess this process. If you celebrate me too much, and I'm not yet capable, I will become frustrated and not do it. If you do too much for me that I can do for myself, I will also become frustrated and not do it.

During dressing time, teach me the difference between "good touches" and "bad touches"—yes, at this age. Create a trust and openness with me so I will tell you immediately if anyone does the "bad touch," and I do mean anyone. I will tell you! I promise I will! Keep me safe, and pay attention!

Development Assignment

Please review the following websites to learn more about my self-help development. Please choose recommended strategies to add to your list of development activities. Review the milestones directly before my age, my age range, and beyond my age range. Example: If I am 12 months, review the milestones for 9-12, 12-15 and 15-18 months, so that you will know what to expect.

American Academy of Pediatrics website

Prenatal
https://www.healthychildren.org/English/ages-stages/prenatal/Pages/default.aspx

Baby
https://www.healthychildren.org/English/ages-stages/baby/Pages/default.aspx

Toddler
https://www.healthychildren.org/English/ages-stages/toddler/Pages/default.aspx

Preschool
https://www.healthychildren.org/English/ages-stages/
preschool/Pages/default.aspx

Gradeschool
https://www.healthychildren.org/English/ages-stages/
gradeschool/Pages/default.aspx

Developmental Milestones of Early Literacy
https://www.healthychildren.org/English/ages-stages/
baby/Pages/Developmental-Milestones-of-Early-Literacy.
aspx

What to Expect website

http://www.whattoexpect.com/milestones/

Zero to Three website

https://www.zerotothree.org/resources/series/your-child-
s-development-age-based-tips-from-birth-to-36-months

Self-Help Assessment

Name_____ Age____

Skills

Follows Routines and Assists

First Attempt

How Often?

Concerns

Sleeps in Own Bed

First Attempt

How Often?

Concerns

Sleeps through the Night

First Attempt

How Often?

Concerns

Breastfeeds

First Attempt

How Often?

Concerns

Stops Breastfeeding

First Attempt

How Often?

Concerns

Reaches for Bottle

First Attempt

How Often?

Concerns

Holds Bottle with Assistance

First Attempt

How Often?

Concerns

Holds Bottle all By Myself

First Attempt

How Often?

Concerns

Eats Baby Food from Spoon

First Attempt

How Often?

Concerns

Decreased Consumption of Milk or Formula

First Attempt

How Often?

Concerns

Eats Table Food with Hands

First Attempt

How Often?

Concerns

Tolerates a Variety of Foods

First Attempt

How Often?

Concerns

Safely Chews and Swallows a Wider Variety of Textured Foods

First Attempt

How Often?

Concerns

Uses Spoon with Hand-over-Hand Assistance

First Attempt

How Often?

Concerns

Uses Spoon all by Myself

First Attempt

How Often?

Concerns

Uses Fork all by Myself

First Attempt

How Often?

Concerns

Transitions from Bottle to Sippy Cup

First Attempt

How Often?

Concerns

Hand-over-Hand Assistance Sippy Cup

First Attempt

How Often?

Concerns

Bye-Bye Bottle Ceremony

First Attempt

How Often?

Concerns

Transitions from Sippy Cup to Open Cup

First Attempt

How Often?

Concerns

Cries when Diaper Wet or Soiled

First Attempt

How Often?

Concerns

Given and Repeats Name for Urination

First Attempt

How Often?

Concerns

Given and Repeats Name for Bowel Movement

First Attempt

How Often?

Concerns

Assists with Diaper Changes

First Attempt

How Often?

Concerns

Informs of Wet or Soiled Diaper

First Attempt

How Often?

Concerns

Potty-Training Preparation Conversations

First Attempt

How Often?

Concerns

Listens to Potty Book Story Multiple Times

First Attempt

How Often?

Concerns

Sits on Toilet for One Minute, Supervised

First Attempt

How Often?

Concerns

Gets New Potty Seat for Toilet or Chair for Floor

First Attempt

How Often?

Concerns

Gets New Underwear

First Attempt

How Often?

Concerns

Gets Elmo Watch (Optional)

First Attempt

How Often?

Concerns

Sits on Toilet or Potty Chair for One Minute, Supervised and Does Urination or Bowel Movement

First Attempt

How Often?

Concerns

Informs of Need to Use Toilet or Potty

First Attempt

How Often?

Concerns

Uses Potty Independently

First Attempt

How Often?

Concerns

Participates in Tooth Brushing

First Attempt

How Often?

Concerns

Lifts Body Parts to Assist during Dressing

First Attempt

How Often?

Concerns

Takes Clothes Off (shoes, socks, pants, shirt, underwear)

First Attempt

How Often?

Concerns

Puts Clothes On (underwear, shirt, pants, socks, shoes)

First Attempt

How Often?

Concerns

Questions for Pediatrician

"A child who is allowed to be disrespectful to his parents will not have true respect for anyone."

—Billy Graham

"Taking the child's point of view demands good will, time, and effort on the part of parents. The child is the clear beneficiary. Parents who make the effort to understand their children's point of view are likely to treat children fairly and in an age-appropriate manner."

—David Elkind

Your Thoughts:

Chapter 8

Guiding Behavior Development —Support Me

Guiding a child's behavior involves supporting the child's development in a positive and encouraging way (Martin & Berke, 2007).

Behavior and Areas of Development

Your focus must be on guiding my behavior. Your success or failure in this area is connected to your success or failure in the other developmental areas. If you don't take control of this behavioral area, I will. I will determine your response to my behavior and whether you respond at all. I will determine whether you raise your voice and the level you raise it. Focus—there will be a shift in me around 12 months, and it will develop momentum through 35.9 months. It's something about being able to walk around on my own that makes me feel powerful. Even if you tell me to sit down, and I do it, my insides will be standing up.

Parents and caregivers, as you read this handbook, please realize your language, physical, cognitive, social-emotional, and self-help skills are directly related to mine. You teach me the language that you use. You teach me what you know and what you don't know. You teach by how you interact with me and others and how you manage your own emotions. Your ability to teach independence is directly connected to what you think I can and cannot do.

I will learn your behavioral guidance strategies (if you have any) better than you. I study. Many people think because I am so young that I am not aware. I am aware of everything. I am experiencing everything, and if you don't adjust my thinking, I'll have to do it myself. I respond to everything. Watch my responses. Go ahead of me and guide—don't get behind me. If you lead from behind, you will spend the rest of my developmental stages trying to catch up. One day, you will wake up and realize that you are not in charge at all. I am!

Here is an example of how to get ahead of me and guide. If there is a behavior that I am engaging in that will not be appropriate at 6, 16, or 26 years of age, do not let me engage in it at 12, 18, or 24 months of age. Example: Standing in the chair may look cute at 12, 18, or 24 months, but it will be inappropriate at 6, 16, and 26 years of age. Please don't laugh at what you think is cute now. It will make you cry later.

Any inappropriate behaviors I engage in will escalate if I am given positive attention for them. It is very difficult to correct inappropriate behaviors that are allowed. Perform an "across-setting test" to see if the behaviors I am exhibiting at home will be appropriate in any setting outside the home.

Please allow me to engage in positive behaviors with the family as my audience. Encourage me to do the following: sing the "*ABC* Song," sing and do the movements for "Itsy, Bitsy Spider," read my favorite book that I have already requested you to read fifty times, tell a made-up story, display my artwork, and so on. There are many positive activities of engagement that will build my self-esteem and set the course of my life on a positive track.

As with everything, *balance* is the key. Teach me that I will not always have an audience and that sometimes I will need to be the audience. Teach me the proper actions of performer and audience member so I will know how to conduct myself in either role. If you don't teach me, I may reverse the roles at inappropriate times.

If I engage in positive behaviors from birth, I will have years to practice before I reach adulthood. If I engage in negative behaviors from birth, I will also have years to practice before I reach adulthood. Remember, what goes in comes out. Positive in equals positive out, and negative in equals negative out. Help me and you will help the world.

The External Environment and Me

The external environment will have a lot of influence on the development of my behavior. The places I go, people I interact with, and things I see will all influence my behavior. My inner person who thinks, feels, interprets, sees, and comprehends may at times be in direct opposition to the external environment. At times, the external environment will be in direct opposition to my inner person. I need you to guide my behavior and help me to get to the level where I can guide it myself. At this stage, I absorb everything like a sponge. Oftentimes, you will wonder where I learned this or that. Keep track of my input because my output will show what and how I processed things that I learned.

Guide My Ability to Think and Reason

Please guide my ability to think and reason. This ability will help me guide my own behavior. My negative behavior is a direct result of my negative thinking. As well, my positive behavior is a direct result of my positive thinking. Get into the gap between the two, and start your work from here.

Especially take note of how well I follow commands and instructions. Carefully watch my physical response when I am told what to do. Do my eyes roll? Do my shoulders shrug? Do I look the other way while you are talking to me? Do I appear to not be listening? If so, stop here and figure out why these behaviors are present. The behaviors might be present because you have not established your authority as the parent. If you don't figure it out, these behaviors will evolve to the point where neither you nor I will be able to control them. They will become habit, and bad habits are hard to break. Please help me!

If you give me instructions one time and I don't listen, you are going to think I didn't hear you and say them again. I heard you, and I'm not going to listen when you say them again. If you say it five times, I will continue to not do what I am told. I will decide whether I am going to do it at all. Pay attention. This is a crucial aspect of my child development and where behavioral guidance is needed.

Go back to the basics. Stop—take a couple of breaths. Look—are there any signs of frustration or anger in me or you? Listen—am I asking or pleading for help without your knowing? Observe me; watch my body language. Be here for me. Empower me to self-evaluate, self-soothe, and de-escalate. Always reassure me. I need you more than ever during this challenging period of my life. Don't give up on me. We will get through this together.

The Art of Manipulation

I have been studying you for two years and have learned the art of manipulation. I have learned how to get a reaction out of you. Your reaction is engagement with me to stop the behavior through an (effective or ineffective) behavioral guidance strategy. I have calculated what your responses will be to almost all my behavioral interactions. I also know that if I keep pushing, you will always give in and give me whatever I want. I always seek to control your behavior; I already know I'm not big enough to control you. I'm not the problem—my behavior is.

Self-Regulation

Please teach me how to regulate my own emotions without the use of external regulators. Self-regulation is a skill I will need to master and use the rest of my life. This is my ability to follow rules without adult direction. When I struggle with my emotions, ask me how I feel. At times, I may need you to define the emotion for me, starting at birth. You can say things like I see you're feeling sad, mad, happy, tired, cranky, and so on. Please provide me with *constructive outlet choices*. These are choices that will help me develop or improve my behavior.

Your care and concern about my emotional well-being will allow me the courage to distance myself from you and enable me to deal with my many emotions in a constructive manner. I will eventually be able to independently choose constructive outlets.

The Temper Tantrum

I have continued to study and now have a wealth of experience. It's not hard to figure me out—I want my way, I will try to get my way, and try to get you to do what I want. Don't look at me; look at my behaviors.

There's a thing called a *temper tantrum*. (I discussed it in the social-emotional chapter. I need to continue to discuss it here because understanding this will help you to guide my behavior.) This is one of the main techniques I use to control. When I'm told no, I let out a gut-wrenching scream. I don't need tears because the scream usually gets me what I want. If you don't respond quickly enough, I will then use my body. I will position myself on the floor, kick my legs, and stomp my feet. My face is in this contorted shape. My mouth is opening and closing at will. Oh, and by the way, I add tears for an even greater effect. If you ignore me, I get louder.

I coordinate all this, and I watch as you slowly weaken and give me what I asked you for in the first place. Why didn't you just give it to me when I asked so I wouldn't have to go through all of this? I will always try to get you to do what I say and want because I want control, and this control could possibly begin before I reach the age of two.

Remember this awful tantrum, because I will use it again.

It is very important at this phase to keep distance between us. You must use your body as an instructional tool. Your torso becomes the instruction board where I can read every message. Your arms become the markers that have different meanings depending on their position—outstretched, used one at a time, folded across your chest, or placed on your hips. Pick a meaning for each and use it the same way each time you are guiding my behavior.

If you don't use your body as an instructional tool and create and maintain distance, I will close the gap and use your own body to control you. I will do this by pushing my body against yours, intensify my cry, and raise my arms to be picked up. Once you pick me up, I will lock my body into yours and bury my face in your chest or arms. This will cause lack of eye contact that aids in communication. I can even make you sit or stand, depending on how I thrust my body.

Sitting or standing, I am weakening your back and torso. In this position, I am also tugging at your heart strings and weakening your resolve. I am rendering you powerless to stop this undesirable behavior. When you attempt to remove me from the area, I will tighten my body around your torso. This will help to weaken your legs, because now you must walk with me clinging to your body. I lift my head at times to block your vision so that, in extreme cases, you will lose your balance and make us both fall. You now leave wherever we are in utter shame and disgrace because you didn't have the power to stop me.

Characteristics of Effective and Ineffective Strategies for Guiding Behavior

There are strategies that you can use to guide my behavior. Some strategies are effective and some are ineffective, but both kinds are directly connected to whether you believe that I understand or do not understand instructions and commands. The characteristics of these strategies have been compiled into a chart on the following page. Please review them now. In a future handbook, we will review all the components that make the strategies effective or ineffective.

Effective Strategies	Ineffective Strategies
Provides Clear Understanding of Authority	No Clear Understanding of Authority
Strict	Lenient
Cannot Be Manipulated	Easily Manipulated
Consistent	Inconsistent
Self-Controlled	Child Controlled
Calm and Self-Assured	Overwhelmed
Says Things One Time, Expects Results and Gets Results	Says Things Multiple Times, Doesn't Expect Results, Doesn't Get Results
Anticipates Previous Challenges and Makes Plan for Prevention	Doesn't Anticipate Previous Challenges and Does Not Make Plan for Prevention
Self-Evaluates Strategies; Uses What Works and Discards What Does Not	Never Self-Evaluates Strategies; Uses Strategies that Don't Work
Seeks Evaluation from Others Regarding Own Behavior in Relation to Child	Seeks Evaluation from Others Regarding Child's Behavior
Establishes Effective Consequences	Establishes Ineffective Consequences

Effective Strategies	Ineffective Strategies
Provides Explanation of How Consequences Are Connected to Behavior	Does Not Provide Explanation of How Consequences Are Connected to Behavior
Matches Consequences to Personality and Developmental Level of Child	Does Not Consider the Personality or Developmental Level of Child when Establishing Consequences
Focuses on Child	Focuses on Others
Helps Child Gain Self-Control	Helps Child to Be Controlled by Others
Does Not Seek Approval from Child	Seeks Approval from Child
Enjoys Time with Child	Time with Child Is Stressful

The Three Rs of Behavior

The three Rs of behavior are: *recognition, reaction,* and *response.* The three Rs happen during my interaction with others. There are two unique perspectives:

From your perspective:

1) *Recognition* is that you notice my behavior.

2) *Reaction* is your engagement with me to stop the behavior through an (effective or ineffective) behavioral guidance strategy.

3) *Response* is what you do after the undesirable behavior stops or continues.

From my perspective:

1) *Recognition* is that I see you notice my behavior.

2) *Reaction* is my engagement with you as you implement the (effective or ineffective) behavioral guidance strategy.

3) *Response* is my choice to stop or continue the undesirable behavior.

Please use recognition, reaction, and response to help me achieve the goal of self-control.

Recognition is the most critical component because your timeliness will determine the effectiveness of my reaction and response. There must be a shift in your demeanor and tone from play mode to stern as you guide my behavior. You will send mixed messages if you continue to use the same tone, play with me, and smile as you guide my behavior. You will need to have a repertoire of effective strategies that will ensure I stop undesirable behaviors in response to your authority.

I need to be able to recognize approval or disapproval. I need to respond to redirection when angry or frustrated and behave appropriately without having temper tantrums. As you engage me in the three Rs, I will eventually use more positive ways to calm myself. In a future handbook, we will use the three Rs strategy with the effective and ineffective strategies from the prior characteristic chart. I have provided some effective strategies in the next section that you may begin using immediately.

Ways to Gain Compliance Using Positive Behavior Guidance Strategies

With guidance strategies, the child learns self-control and is empowered to operate independently; with discipline, the child learns who is boss and who holds the power in the relationship—and it's not the child (Martin & Berke, 2007).

Compliance is obedience. I need to know what to obey, how to obey, and who to obey. There will be many authority figures whom I will interact with throughout life. These foundational obedience strategies that I learn now will help me to follow rules throughout my life. Remember that resistance and temper tantrums are my way of communicating my independence. At these stages of my development, use positive behavior guidance techniques. Always *explain the expectations of behavior* in all situations, and when I comply, tell me that I complied and how amazing I am. This is one way to catch me doing the right thing. I will then want to impress even more by doing more things right.

Another strategy is to use *redirection* as much as possible. This is when you turn my attention to a more desirable activity. Do not offer a reward for good behavior because if you do, I will behave for the reward. I might also begin to not care about a reward and still engage in negative behavior. The absence of a reward will help me to develop an internal mechanism in which I will do the right thing because it is the right thing to do. If you do it this way, it will build my self-esteem.

Time-out is a popular strategy. Please use it wisely between the ages of eighteen and thirty-six months. Please use it with supervision and without. To use it effectively, I must understand your authority and have a loving, caring relationship with you. For supervised time-out, remove me from playing with my toys and sit with me. Restate in a few words why the time-out is given. Tell me that the two of us are going to watch the toys play by themselves. Sit quietly with me for about one minute. Then emphatically state, "Okay, I think you're ready now." Ask me if I'm ready, and watch me enthusiastically say yes. I can't wait to get back to playing with you and my toys. My toys were looking very sad.

As the two of us return to play, explain that if the behavior occurs again, you will go with me to time out again. Praise me when I exhibit appropriate behavior. Immediately return with me to time-out if the inappropriate behavior occurs again. Do this a maximum of three times, and then choose a new strategy. For time-out without supervision, use the same strategies as supervised time-out. Please don't go to time-out with me for this one. Instruct me to sit quietly for one to two minutes.

Another way to gain my compliance is to **explain to me that you know how challenging it is to do what you say.** Tell me you admire how I am doing it. Tell me often, and when you see I have mastered a particularly challenging behavior, don't continue to say it. Move to another area of challenge and begin all over again. When I engage in positive behavior, give me positive feedback and helpful praise. When I engage in negative behavior, provide an explanation of the negative behavior and a clear expectation of the desired behavior. Give praise only after I comply. Expect me to do the right thing and watch me do it.

Please set up **consequences** for noncompliant behavior. I function best when boundaries are set and maintained. Please include me in setting up the consequences—yes, even at two years old. Remember, if you have already established the expectations of behavior, I will now understand consequences.

Ask me what consequence I would like when I don't comply. This will remove you out of the role of authoritarian and move me into the role of self-regulation. In the beginning, I am going to give a consequence of not playing with the toy that is my least favorite. Ha, ha, I still tried to get you. It is not a consequence if you take something from me that I don't deeply desire. Remember my age, developmental level, and personality—sometimes the mere removal of your attention and engagement will be enough to gain compliance.

Another strategy that you could use is a **counting system.** When you get to a certain number, a consequence that I don't like must happen. Three is a good number because if you stretch it out to five, that will give me more time to engage in the inappropriate behavior. If I start counting along with you instead of rushing to stop the behavior, you know this is an ineffective strategy for my personality.

One of the most effective strategies is to offer me *choices*. The thing that makes this strategy so effective is that it seems like I am choosing. You are making the two choices and then offering them to me. Any choice that I make will be acceptable because you strategically designed the choices. I will think I am in control when you are. Remember, though, certain behaviors must never have choices as an option.

Another strategy that is not often listed or discussed is *"The Look."* This strategy must be used correctly for it to work. Before the use of this strategy, you must have a very caring and trusting relationship with me in which I comply most of the time. I must have a firm understanding and respect of your authority as the parent.

"The Look" is a nonverbal communication method in which you look intently at me, without any facial expression, while I am in the process of an inappropriate behavior. This strategy can only be used if you have verbally corrected me prior to this. You lock eyes with me, and I in turn lock eyes with you. You communicate to stop the undesirable behavior just by the look. I receive the message clearly and stop the undesirable behavior immediately and make a better choice to engage in appropriate behaviors. You then return to whatever you were doing. There is never any discussion about this after it occurs.

Finally, the most effective strategy is embedded in my routines. It is called **structure**. Review the routines in the self-help chapter. I will engage more productively when I know what will come next. This will help me predict and plan. I also learn how to tell time. Participation in routines will help you to observe, monitor, and address the areas of challenge not only for me but also for yourself. Do things the same way, in the same order, and at the same time for every routine.

Take special note of transitions. **Transitions** are the times that I change from one routine to another. Organize these. Use five-minute warnings, countdowns, timers, bells, whistles, microphones, pictures of the parts of the routine, questions about what comes next, and songs. Be creative. You will know you have achieved success when I inform you that it is nap time and prepare myself without your assistance. Over time, I will do this for all my routines. Every routine is preparation for my independence.

Most of all, remember, it is easier to gain compliance when you have built a *lasting, committed, and loving relationship* with me. It is easier to guide my behavior when you *spend more time praising than criticizing*. It is also easier when you are *consistent*—say what you mean and mean what you say. When you deal with me from feelings of *love and compassion*, you teach me how to display these traits with you and others. Our love for each other will ensure that we both want the best for each other and will help us both get through this challenging child development time. Thank you for helping me!

"The education of even a small child, therefore, does not aim at preparing him for school, but for life."

—Maria Montessori

Your Thoughts:

Concluding Remarks

Here is a capsule version of child development. I took the time out to share all of this to help everyone who engages with me at this stage of my development. Remember to engage me in all areas of receptive and expressive language development, gross and fine motor physical development, cognitive, social-emotional, and self-help development. Guiding my behavior is the key to successfully engaging me in all areas of development. Prepare me for life! Prepare me for life!

If you notice any delay in any of the areas of my development, please speak to my pediatrician and/or call your state's early intervention service. The early intervention service will identify whether I have a developmental delay in any of the following five areas of development: language, physical, cognitive, social-emotional, or self-help development. The early intervention service will provide a free evaluation, and if I qualify, send a therapist to help us. The services are free and offered birth to three years, or birth to five years, depending on the state in which we live.

Center for Disease Control (CDC)
Baby Steps: "Learn the Signs. Act Early."
https://www.youtube.com/watch?time_
continue=3&v=9Ithxd5KWhw

Early Intervention Contacts United States,
Commonwealths and Territories
https://www.cdc.gov/ncbddd/actearly/parents/states.html

"Children are human beings to whom respect is due, superior to us by reason of their innocence and of the greater possibilities of their future."

—Maria Montessori

Your Thoughts:

"What we see changes what we know. What we know changes what we see."

—Jean Piaget

Your Thoughts:

Afterword

Dear Reader,

This handbook was written to assist everyone who aids in the development of infants and toddlers. It should be used as a guide to engage infants and toddlers in all areas of child development: receptive and expressive language development, gross and fine motor physical development, cognitive, social-emotional, and self-help development. The developmental areas overlap each other. Activities that you engage your child in under one area of development could also be covering other developmental areas. As development activities are created, use the knowledge of the development areas to determine how many areas can be addressed with one activity. The positive behavioral guidance strategies should be used to assist in toddlers' self-regulation of behavior. There is so much to teach. With the information from this handbook, infants and toddlers can be engaged in higher levels of learning that will guide their development. Please read the included companion guide to this handbook, *Let Me Teach You, Baby*, to your infant or toddler.

Use the age ranges in the developmental domains as guides, and remember: Infants and toddlers vary in their developmental time frames. Also, use the developmental domain assessments at the end of each chapter. Completing the development assignments will increase your knowledge of child development. It takes a whole village to develop well-adjusted children. Let's hold each other accountable and strengthen our nation, states, cities, communities, and the institutions that serve and support families and homes. The future of our children and grandchildren depend upon this. As we all prepare children for life, we must *handle them with care!*

I'll see you at home and in institutions that serve infants and toddlers.

—Dr. Scipio

"Parents are in the present and given a present to raise our future."

—Vonda Scipio

References

Books

Martin, S., & Berke, J. *Infants and Toddler: See How They Grow.* Clifton Park, NY: Thomson Delmar Learning, 2007.

Murkoff, H., & Mazel, S. *What to Expect the First Year,* 3rd Edition. New York: Workman Publishing, 2014.

What to Expect the Second Year from 12 to 24 Months. New York, NY: Workman Publishing, 2014.

Shelov, S. P., Altmann, T. R., & Hannemann, R. E. *American Academy of Pediatrics, The Complete and Authoritative Guide Caring for Your Baby and Young Child, Birth to Age 5,* New and Revised Sixth Edition. New York: Bantam Books, 2014.

Quotes Listed throughout the Book: www.azquotes.com

Stevie Wonder: "Isn't She Lovely?"
www.azlyrics.com/lyrics/steviewonder/isntshelovely.html

New Jersey Birth-3 Early Learning Standards
www.nj.gov/eduation/ece/guide/standards/birth/standards.pdf

Tennessee Revised Early Learning Developmental

Standards Birth-48 months

https://tn.gov/assets/entities/education/attachments/
std_tnelds_birth-4yo.pdf

Virginia's Foundation Blocks for Early Learning:
Comprehensive Standards for Four-Year-Olds

www.doe.virginia.gov/instruction/early_childhood/
preschool.../foundationblocks.pdf

Resources

Suggested Materials

These materials have been listed under specific developmental domains and can be used across domain areas. They are suggested, not required. Some items are repeated under different domains. This list is not comprehensive. Please add your favorite materials if they are not listed. The materials are not listed by age range. Please use the appropriate materials for your child's age.

Suggested Language Materials

Books, books on tape and CD; cards with environmental signs; chalk, chalkboard; crayons, felt pens; labels, logos; music on tape and CD; paper; picture cards; pictures (of family members, familiar people, actions, events); pencils; photo library.

Add Your Own Language Materials Below:

Suggested Physical Materials

Barrel; bean bags; blocks; books; bowling pins; bucket; buttons; chalk child-size chair; climbing bars; coffee table; crayons; doll carriage; grocery cart; hoop; incline; jungle gym; lid on jar; low shelf; markers; nuts-and-bolts toy; pens; plates; push-button telephone; push toys; riding toys with pedals and without; rope; sight-and-sound tubes; slide; small cars; sofa; soft and washable sensory balls; spoon; squeakers; stairs; sticks; three-inch large ball; toys that make noise and light up; tricycle; tummy time mat; tunnel; water faucet knob.

Add Your Own Physical Materials Below

Suggested Cognitive Materials

Activity mat; animals; bath toys; beads to string; car and toy garage; books; chain links; containers with objects; counting bears; dishes (cups, plates, pots and pans, utensils); doll and toy bed; dramatic play objects; keys; legos; mechanical toys (jack-in-the-box, objects with handle or string, radio, see-and-say, talking doll, windup toys; mobile, multiple-piece puzzles with knobs and without; people figures; music box; musical instruments; nesting rings; paint; piano; pictures; play dough; play food; pop beads; pull apart and pop together beads; push-and-pull toys; push-button telephone; rattles; sand; shape sorter; simple puzzles with knobs and without; songs; squeeze toys; stairs; tinker toys; vehicles (cars, buses, trucks, airplanes, trains); water play.

Add Your Own Cognitive Materials Below:

Suggested Social-Emotional Materials

Balls, bath toys, blocks, books, buildings, cars, dolls, feelings picture chart, finger plays, musical toys, puppets, push-button telephone, stuffed animals, unbreakable mirrors.

Add Your Own Social-Emotional Materials Below:

Suggested Self-Help Materials

Applesauce, baby monitor, bassinet, books, bowl, breads, child-size table and chairs, coat, crib, cup, fork, fruits, hat, high chair, jacket, milk, meats, pants, shirt, sink, soap, socks, shoes, spoon, toothbrush, toothpaste, towel, training seat or potty chair, tub, vegetables, water, yogurt.

Add Your Own Self-Help Materials Below:

Suggested Books

Nolte, D. L. & Harris, R. *Children Learn What They Live: Parenting to Inspire Values.* New York: Workman Publishing, 1998.

Tsabary, S. *The Conscious Parent: Transforming Ourselves, Empowering Our Children.* Vancouver, Canada: Namaste Publishing, 2010.

Add Your Own Parenting Books Below:

Suggested Baby Albums

My Baby's First Year. New York: Ryland, Peters & Small, 2015.

Baby to Five: An Early Years Journal. New York: Ryland, Peters & Small, 2016.

Helpful Websites

American Academy of Pediatrics
https://www.aap.org/

Your Baby's Temperament
https://www.healthychildren.org/English/ages-stages/
baby/Pages/Babys-Temperament.aspx

Emotional and Social Development: 4 to 7 months
https://www.healthychildren.org/English/ages-stages/
baby/Pages/Emotional-and-Social-Development-4-7-
Months.aspx

Prenatal
https://www.healthychildren.org/English/ages-stages/
prenatal/Pages/default.aspx

Baby
https://www.healthychildren.org/English/ages-stages/
baby/Pages/default.aspx

Toddler
https://www.healthychildren.org/English/ages-stages/
toddler/Pages/default.aspx

Preschool
https://www.healthychildren.org/English/ages-stages/
preschool/Pages/default.aspx

Gradeschool
https://www.healthychildren.org/English/ages-stages/
gradeschool/Pages/default.aspx

Developmental Milestones of Early Literacy
https://www.healthychildren.org/English/ages-stages/
baby/Pages/Developmental-Milestones-of-Early-Literacy.
aspx

Center for Disease Control and Prevention (CDC)
Baby Steps: "Learn the Signs. Act Early."
Video. https://www.youtube.com/watch?time_
continue=3&v=9Ithxd5KWhw

Developmental Milestones
https://www.cdc.gov/ncbddd/actearly/

Developmental Milestones Checklists
https://www.cdc.gov/ncbddd/actearly/pdf/checklists/
all_checklists.pdf

Early Intervention Contacts United States,
Commonwealths and Territories
www.cdc.gov/ncbddd/actearly/parents/states.html

Dr. Shefali Tsabary
https://drshefali.com/

Reach out and Read
www.reachoutandread.org/

Online Encyclopedia of Early Childhood Development
http://www.child-encyclopedia.com

Types of books that children like
https://www.reachoutandread.org/FileRepository/
WhatChildrenLikeinBooks.pdf

Sesame Street: Usher's "*ABC* Song"—YouTube
https://www.youtube.com/watch?v=SWvBAQf7v8g

What to Expect
https://www.whattoexpect.com

Milestones
http://www.whattoexpect.com/milestones/

Zero to Three Organization-Early Connections Last a Lifetime
http://www.zerotothree.org

Milestones
https://www.zerotothree.org/resources/series/your-child-s-development-age-based-tips-from-birth-to-36-months

Add Your Own Websites Below:

Suggested Children's Book List

(This list is not comprehensive. Please add your favorite titles). All books can be found on Amazon. Please check your local library or book stores and read books of interest before purchase.

All of Baby Nose to Toes, Victoria Adler

A You're Adorable, Martha Alexander

Clifford Goes to Dog School, Norman Bridwell

Clifford the Big Red Dog, Norman Bridwell

A to Z, Sandra Boynton

Barnyard Dance, Sandra Boynton

Blue Hat, Green Hat, Sandra Boynton

Doggies, Sandra Boynton

The Going to Bed Book, Sandra Boynton

Good Night Moon, Margaret Wise Brown

Whose Baby Am I?, John Butler

Dear Zoo, Rod Campbell

The Very Hungry Caterpillar, Eric Carle

Five Little Monkeys Jumping on the Bed, Eileen Christelow

My First Songs, Tomie dePaola

Llama, Llama Home with Mama, Anna Dewdney

Llama, Llama Mad at Mama, Anna Dewdney

Llama, Llama Misses Mama, Anna Dewdney

Llama Red Pajama, Anna Dewdney

Llama, Llama and the Bully Goat, Anna Dewdney

Honey Baby Sugar Child, Alice Faye Duncan

Your Baby's First Word Will Be DaDa, Jimmy Fallon

Corduroy, Don Freeman

Corduroy Goes to the Doctor, Don Freeman

Spot Goes to the Library, Eric Hill

Where's Spot?, Eric Hill

ABC Look at Me, Roberta Grobel Intrater

Peekaboo Morning, Rachel Isadora

Where Is Baby's Belly Button?, Karen Katz

Counting Kisses, Karen Katz

No Biting, Karen Katz

Head, Shoulders, Knees, and Toes, Annie Kubler

Ten Little Monkeys Jumping on the Bed, Annie Kubler and Tina Freeman

Look, Look!, Peter Linenthal

Look at the Animals, Peter Linenthal

Chicka Chicka Boom Boom, Bill Martin and John Archambault

Brown Bear, Brown Bear, What Do You See? Bill Martin Jr. /Eric Carle

Polar Bear, Polar Bear, What Do You Hear? Bill Martin Jr. /Eric Carle

Winnie the Pooh's Opposites, A.A. Milne

My Farm Friends, Wendell Minor

Potty, Leslie Patricelli

Where's My Nose?, Susan Ring and Stephanie Peterson

Good Night Gorilla, Peggy Rathmann

Truck Stop, Anne Rockwell

Little Blue Truck, Alice Schertle and Jill McElmurry

The Cheerios Play Book, Lee Wade

If You're Happy and You Know It (Jungle Edition), James Warhola

Happy, Pharrell Williams

The House that Jack Built, Jeanette Winter

The Napping House, Audrey Wood and Don Wood

Add Your Own Titles Below:

COMPANION GUIDE

Let Me Teach *You*, Baby

How to Help Infants and Toddlers Grow and Develop Literacy Skills

Dr. Vonda K. Scipio, Ed.D.

Dedication

To all the wonderful infants
and toddlers of the world.

Table of Contents

Introduction

Parents and caregivers, please use this collection of fun photographs and cute poems to engage your infants and toddlers in optimum development while teaching important language skills, as well as gross and fine motor physical, cognitive, social-emotional, and self-help in the domains of child development. It includes literacy research, strategies, and checklists for books, songs, play, and materials. Shared reading is an activity that caregivers and children can do for pleasure. During shared reading, caregivers and children can enjoy the language and content of stories and the accompanying illustrations.

Instructions for Using the Companion Guide

1. Review the research.

2. Read each page to infants and toddlers and show pictures.

3. At the appropriate age, engage infants and toddlers in the developmental milestone on each page. (Use Part I, *Let Babies Teach: Learning Child Development through Observing Infants and Toddlers,* for age ranges.)

4. Use the suggested books, songs, play exercises, and materials to engage infants and toddlers in language, gross and fine motor physical, cognitive, social-emotional, and self-help skills. Add your own books, songs, play, exercises, and materials to the suggested lists.

5. Review the literacy strategies in prescription forms. Add your own literacy strategies.

6. Use the positive behavioral guidance strategies. Add your own positive behavioral guidance strategies.

7. Make up your own stories about the infants and toddlers on each page.

8. Choose literacy strategies to begin using immediately.

Research

In 2004, the United Nations Educational, Scientific, and Cultural Organization (UNESCO) defined literacy as follows:

Literacy is the ability to identify, understand, interpret, create, communicate, compute, and use printed and written materials associated with varying contexts. Literacy involves a continuum of learning in enabling individuals to achieve their goals, to develop their knowledge and potential, and to participate fully in their community and wider society (UNESCO, 2004, p. 13). The first three years are "incredibly important in producing a nation of readers" (Rosenkoetter & Knapp-Philo, 2004, p. 5).

Family Literacy is viewed as the source of three broad categories of literacy experiences for young children: (1) experiences in which children interact with their parents in writing and reading situations; (2) experiences in which children explore print on their own; and (3) experiences in which children observe their parents modeling literate behaviors when they read or write themselves (Teale & Sulzby, 1986).

Literacy-rich environments contain essential components (e.g., books, daily reading, adult role models, writing materials, etc.) that help foster and support the acquisition of literacy (Martin & Berke, 2007). Per Jalongo (2004) and Vukelich, Christie, and Enz (2002), literacy-rich environments have the following characteristics:

1. Children are surrounded with oral language, books, and print.

2. Book reading to children is an activity that occurs multiple times every day.

3. Reading and writing materials are available; adults model reading and writing as part of their daily routine and activities.

4. TV viewing is not available to infants and toddlers and is closely monitored for preschoolers.

5. Adults support literacy acquisition by answering questions through pointing out print, reading, visiting the library, and providing varied experiences rich in opportunities for learning about the world—such as trips to the parks, museums, and local points of interest.

6. Playing with language and linking play experiences with books and print is supported.

Language

Children develop a sense of the sound structure of language by saying rhymes, singing, reciting finger plays, and clapping the syllables to chanted words (Adams, 1990).

Adult-child conversations are robustly associated with healthy language development. Parents should be encouraged not merely to provide language input to their children through reading or storytelling but also to engage their children in two-sided conversations (Zimmerman, Gilkerson, Richards, Christakis, Xu, Gray & Yapanel, 2009).

Children acquire vocabulary, other language skills, and background knowledge about many topics by participating in frequent, meaningful conversations with responsive adults; such conversations contribute to early reading success (Dickinson & Tabors, 2001).

Children also must learn the social rules of communicating—being polite, speaking so the listener understands, and taking turns; social rules often vary from culture to culture and from one community to another (Trawick-Smith, 2006).

Strong language skills are essential for children's success in school and life (Hart & Risley, 2003), and one of the best predictors of educational and life-skills competency is the level to which a child progresses in reading and writing (Neuman, Copple, & Bredekamp, 2000).

Reading

Children who engage in frequent activities with books have larger, more literate vocabularies and learn to read better than children who have few book experiences (Dickinson & Tabors, 1991).

Children follow a typical progression in learning to read storybooks, from pointing and labeling pictures to talking about the pictures to using known words, letter, sound knowledge, and pictures to make meaning of text (Sulzby, 1985).

Print

Knowledge of print concepts develops through direct contact with books and explicit modeling by skilled readers as well as through exposure to environmental print (Adams, 1990).

Literacy Prescription R_x

- Read to your babies while they are in the womb and when they arrive into the world.

Literacy Prescription R_x

- Encourage your child to read to you.

- Continue to read, even if your child appears uninterested.

Literacy Prescription R_x

- Make every literacy encounter fun.

Language Development

You need to talk.
It begins with a coo.
You can depend on me
to help you.

Literacy Strategies

Book Title	Author	I Have Read These Books to My Infant or Toddler	Date
Where's Spot?	Eric Hill		
My First Songs	Tomie dePaola		
If You're Happy and You Know It (Jungle Edition)	James Warhola		

Music and Movement	I have Engaged my Infant or Toddler in Music and Movement Songs	Date
"If You're Happy and You Know It"		

Materials	I Have Used These Materials With My Infant or Toddler	Date
Pictures of Family Members		
Picture Cards of Familiar Objects		
Pictures of Animals		
Cards with Environmental Signs		
Pictures of Familiar People, Actions, Events		
Labels		
Photo Library		
Musical or Talking Toys		
Toy Telephone		

Literacy Prescription   **Rx**

- Sing the alphabet song. Sing L, M, N, O, P slowly.

- Say the alphabet.

- Show your child the letters, words, and sentences.

- Teach letters and letter sounds.

Gross Motor Physical Development

I need a rhyme
for tummy time.
I'll engage you in this,
and you'll be fine.

Literacy Strategies

Book Title	Author	I Have Read These Books to My Infant or Toddler	Date
Where's My Nose?	Susan Ring/ Stephanie Peterson		
Counting Kisses	Karen Katz		
Look, Look	Peter Linenthal		
All of Baby Nose to Toes	Victoria Adler		
Where Is Baby's Belly Button?	Karen Katz		

Toe Play	I have engaged my infant or toddler in toe play.	Date
"This Little Piggy Went to Market"		

Materials	I Have Used These Materials With My Infant or Toddler	Date
Tummy Time Mat		
Squeaker Toys		
Soft Sensory Balls		
Rattles		
Bells		
Squeeze Toys		
Toy Keys		
Mobile		
Crib Gym		

Literacy Prescription ℞

- Place books into the diaper bag.

- Have a book bag filled with favorite books and other literacy materials when going on outings.

I'll entice you to crawl
down the hall.
Soon you'll walk,
but sometimes you'll fall.

Literacy Strategies

Book Title	Author	I Have Read These Books to My Infant or Toddler	Date
Head, Shoulders, Knees, and Toes	Annie Kubler		

Music and Movement	I have Engaged my Infant or Toddler in Music and Movement Songs	Date
"The Wheels on the Bus"		
"Head, Shoulders, Knees, and Toes"		

Materials	I Have Used These Materials With My Infant or Toddler	Date
Push Toys		
Sofa/Coffee Table		
Stairs		
Jungle Gym		
Sliding Board		
Tunnel Toys		
Climbing Toys		
Doll Carriage		
Grocery Cart		

Literacy Prescription **R**x

- Place books out with toys during your child's play. Your child will have the option of playing with toys and/or reading books.

Fine Motor Physical Development

I'll teach you to use your hands to reach, grasp, drop, bang, retain, and make marks, scribble, place pegs into pegboards, build towers with blocks, paint, and play in the sand.

Literacy Strategies

Book Title	Author	I Have Read These Books to My Infant or Toddler	Date
The Cheerios Play Book	Lee Wade		

Finger Play	I have engaged my infant or toddler in toe play.	Date
"The Itsy, Bitsy Spider"		
"Where Is Thumbkin?"		
"Twinkle, Twinkle Little Star"		

Materials	I Have Used These Materials With My Infant or Toddler	Date
Crayons, Pencils, Pens, Markers		
Chalk and Chalkboard		
Paper		
Toys to Grasp		
Mechanical and Wind-up Toys		
Playdough and Tools		
Paint		
Sand/Water Play		
Puzzles		
Pegs and Pegboards		
Blocks and Legos		
Shape Sorter		
One-Inch Beads		
Half-Inch Beads		
Scissors		

Literacy Prescription   R𝗑

- Provide paper, crayons, pencils, markers, and chalk to engage your child in exploring how literacy works.

- Teach your child to only use writing materials on paper or notebooks.

- Encourage your child to write and then encourage him or her to read the scribble to you.

- Write your child's name and show him or her each letter. Say each letter.

Cognitive Development

I'll read, read, read a book,

I'll read one every day.

Oh, you'll like it, oh you'll like it,

I'll include it in your play.

Literacy Strategies

Books	I Have Read These Books to My Infant or Toddler	Date
Spot Goes to the Library/ Eric Hill		
Picture Books		
Story Books		
Nursery Rhymes		
Poetry Books		
Song Books		
Information Books		

Literacy Prescription ℞

- Read to your child daily.

- Model literate acts in the presence of your child by opening mail, writing grocery lists, and reading books and magazines for your own pleasure.

- Your child will want to read when he sees you read.

- Encourage other family members, friends, siblings, and other children to read to your child.

- Have your child sit in various positions during each story session—on your lap, next to you, facing you, standing, and so on.

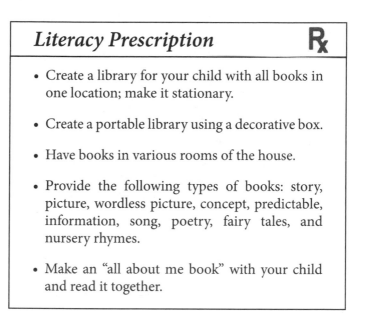

Literacy Prescription   ℞

- Create a library for your child with all books in one location; make it stationary.

- Create a portable library using a decorative box.

- Have books in various rooms of the house.

- Provide the following types of books: story, picture, wordless picture, concept, predictable, information, song, poetry, fairy tales, and nursery rhymes.

- Make an "all about me book" with your child and read it together.

Literacy Prescription   ℞

- Teach your child the proper care of books.

- Teach the parts of a book: front cover, back cover, spine, pages, author, illustrator, etc.

You will say no,

but I won't go.

Through play, I will teach you

letters, numbers, and colors,

and your name you will know.

Literacy Strategies

Book Title	Author	I Have Read These Books to My Infant or Toddler	Date
Good Night, Moon	Margaret Wise Brown		
Peek-A-Boo Morning	Rachel Isadora		
Honey Baby Sugar Child	Alice Faye Duncan		
The House that Jack Built	Jeanette Winter		
Winnie the Pooh Opposites	A. A. Milne		
A to Z	Sandra Boynton		
A, You're Adorable	Martha Alexander		
Doggies	Sandra Boynton		
Five Little Monkeys Jumping on the Bed	Eileen Christelow		
Ten Little Monkeys Jumping on the Bed	Annie Kubler Tina Freeman		
Dear Zoo	Rod Campbell		
Look at the Animals	Peter Linenthal		
Brown Bear, Brown Bear	Bill Martin Jr. /Eric Carle		
Polar Bear, Polar Bear	Bill Martin Jr. /Eric Carle		
Clifford the Big Red Dog	Norman Bridwell		
Clifford Goes to Dog School	Norman Bridwell		
Blue Hat, Green Hat	Sandra Boynton		
Little Blue Truck	Alice Schertle and Jill McElmurry		
Truck Stop	Anne Rockwell		

Songs	I have Engaged my Infant or Toddler in Songs	Date
"The Alphabet Song"		
"Old MacDonald Had a Farm"		
"One, Two, Buckle My Shoe"		
"Songs with Letters"		
"Songs with Numbers"		
"Songs with Colors"		
"Songs to (Insert Name)"		

Materials	I Have Used These Materials With My Infant or Toddler	Date
People Figures		
Counting Bears		
Toys of Various Shapes, Colors, Sizes		
Ring Stacker		
Shape Sorter		

Literacy Prescription ℞

- Have discussions.

- Ask open-ended questions that do not have a correct or incorrect answer.

- Wait for a response and then give the answer.

- Encourage your child to point to pictures in books and point to objects in the environment that match the pictures in books.

- Discuss things in the book while reading.

- Encourage your child to talk and ask questions; this is not an interruption of the story. This helps your child to process the information.

- Encourage your child to read to you.

Social-Emotional Development

Why do you cry?
I don't always know why.
I know your needs,
and meet them I try.

Literacy Strategies

Book Title	Author	I Have Read These Books to My Infant or Toddler	Date
Llama, Llama Red Pajama	Anna Dewdney		
Llama, Llama Mad at Mama	Anna Dewdney		
Llama, Llama Misses Mama	Anna Dewdney		
Llama, Llama and the Bully Goat	Anna Dewdney		
ABC, Look at Me	Roberta Grobel Intrater		

Songs	I have Engaged my Infant or Toddler in Songs	Date
"You Are My Sunshine"		
"Barney Song"		

Play	I have Engaged my Infant or Toddler in Play	Date
Peek-a-Boo		

Materials	I Have Used These Materials With My Infant or Toddler	Date
Books on Tape and CD		
Music on Tape and CD		
Feelings Picture Chart		
Baby Monitor		

Literacy Prescription   ℞

- Obtain more literacy strategies from other caregivers of infants and toddlers.

Self-Help Development

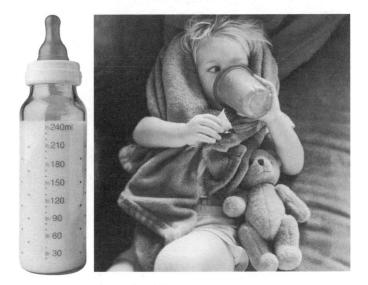

I will not coddle.
I'll assist while you hold your
bottle,
and then over time, bye-bye
bottle.
I'll help you up
to reach your cup.

Literacy Strategies

Materials	I Have Used These Materials With My Infant or Toddler	Date
Bottles		
Sippy Cups		
Open Cups		
Milk		
Water		
Juice		

Literacy Prescription   ℞

- Teach your child to listen, sit quietly, and think. These are skills he will need to use throughout his life.

- Limit the use of technology: television, smart phones, iPads, tablets, and so on.

Potty training on the toilet
or potty chair,
I'll handle with care.
I'll take off the diaper
and get your underwear.

Literacy Strategies

Book Title	Author	I Have Read These Books to My Infant or Toddler	Date
Potty	Leslie Patricelli		

Materials	I Have Used These Materials With My Infant or Toddler	Date
Potty Toilet Seat		
Potty Chair		
Underwear		
Pull-ups for Bedtime		
Elmo Potty Watch		

Literacy Prescription ℞

- Label things in the environment, and read the labels as areas are used.

Literacy Prescription ℞

- Sing many songs together.

- Sing and read the words in books.

- Encourage your child to sing to you.

There's so much to teach
you,
There's so much to learn.
You teach me;
I'll teach you.
We will take turns.

Literacy Strategies

Book Title	Author	I Have Read These Books to My Infant or Toddler	Date
Corduroy	Don Freeman		
Corduroy Goes to the Doctor	Don Freeman		
The Very Hungry Caterpillar	Eric Carle		
Good Night, Gorilla	Peggy Rathmann		
My Farm Friends	Wendell Minor		
Barnyard Dance	Sandra Boynton		
Whose Baby Am I?	John Butler		
The Napping House	Audrey Wood and Don Wood		
Going to Bed Book	Sandra Boynton		
No Biting	Karen Katz		

Materials	I Have Used These Materials With My Infant or Toddler	Date
Bassinet and Crib		
Sofa/Coffee Table		
Applesauce, Yogurt, Vegetables, Fruit		
Meats		
Bread		
Raw Vegetables		
Spoon		
Fork		
Bowl		

Materials	I Have Used These Materials With My Infant or Toddler	Date
Dramatic Play Objects for Pretend		
Doll, Toy Bed, Baby Bottle		
Car and Toy Garage		
Balls		
Ride-On Toys		
Riding Toys with Pedals		
Tricycle		
Pullover Shirt		
Shorts		
Long Pants		
Socks		
Shoes		
Jacket, Coat		
Hat		

Literacy Prescription ℞

- Include multiple sessions with many books

- Take your child to the library and bookstores so she will see many books.

- Read to your child while in the library and bookstore.

- Obtain the children's activities schedule of events from libraries and bookstores, and take your child to events.

Literacy Prescription ℞

- Read books to your child on repeated occasions to provide increased exposure to knowledge.

- Read with passion, change your voice for different characters, and make it fun.

Guiding Behavior Development

I love you ♡

Positive behavioral guidance strategies— expectations, redirection, time-out, "the look," and praise—

will help us both get through
this challenging phase.
Consequences, counting system,
I will not forget choice.
I will use these positive
behavioral guidance strategies
with a kind voice.

I love you, my baby.
I love you, my child.
There is so much to teach you.
It will take a while.

Language, physical, cognitive,
social-emotional, and self-help
skills
include guiding your behavior.

I will, I will.

Love, patience, kindness, and
compassion, too
We will teach each other all our
lives through.

Positive Behavioral Guidancce Strategies	I Have Used Positive Behavioral Guidance Strategies With My Toddler	Date
Expectations		
Redirection		
Supervised Time-Out		
Unsupervised Time-Out		
Praise		
Consequences		
Counting System		
Choice		
Kind Voice		
Love		
Patience		
Kindness		
Compassion		

Blank Literacy Prescription Form Rx

Add your own strategies.

References

Adams, M. J. *Beginning to Read: Thinking and Learning about Print*. Cambridge, MA: MIT Press, 1990.

Dickinson, D. K., & Tabors, P. O. (1991). "Early literacy: Linkages between home, school, and literacy achievement at age five." *Journal of Research in Childhood Education*, 6, 30–46.

———, eds. *Building literacy with language: Young children learning at home and school*. Baltimore, MD: Paul H. Brookes, 2001.

Hart, B., & Risley, T. R. (2003). "The early catastrophe." *Education Review*, 17(1), 110–18.

Jalongo, M. R. *Young Children and Picture Books*. Washington, DC: NAEYC, 2004.

Martin, S., & Berke, J. *See How They Grow: Infants and Toddlers*. Clifton Park, NY: Thomson Delmar Learning, 2007.

Neuman, S., Copple, C., & Bredekamp, S. *Learning to Read and Write: Developmentally Appropriate Practices for Young Children*. Washington, DC: National Association for the Education of Young Children, 2007.

Rosenkoetter, S. E., & Knapp-Philo, J. (2004). "Learning to read the world: Literacy in the first 3 years." *Zero to Three*, 25 (1), 4–9.

Sulzby, E. (1985). "Children's emergent reading of favorite storybooks: A developmental study." *Reading Research Quarterly*, 20(4), 464. International Reading Association.

Teale, W. H., & Sulzby, E. "Emergent Literacy as a Perspective for Examining How Young Children Become Writers and Readers." In W. H. Teale, & E. Sulzby (EDS.), *Emergent Literacy: Writing and Reading* (pp. vii–xxv). Norwood, NJ: Ablex, 1986.

Trawick-Smith, J. *Early Childhood Development: A Multicultural Perspective*. New York: Pearson, 2006.

UNESCO. "The Plurality of Literacy and Its Implications for Policies and Programmes." UNESCO Education Sector position paper. Paris: UNESCO, 2004.

Vulkelich, C., Christie, J. F., & Enz, B. *Helping Young Children Learn Language and Literacy*. Boston: Allyn and Bacon, 2002.

Zimmerman, F. J., Gilkerson, J., Richards, J. A., Christakis, D. A., Xu, D., Gray, S., Yapanel, U. "Teaching by listening: The importance of adult-child conversations to language development." *Pediatrics* 2009; 124;342 DOI: 10.1542/peds.2008-2267.
https://www.researchgate.net/
publication/26328343_Teaching_by_
Listening_The_Importance_of_Adult-Child_
Conversations_to_Language_Development

About the Author

Vonda Scipio, Ed.D., has been an advocate for children and families for eighteen years. She holds a doctorate in education with a focus on instruction and curriculum leadership and a concentration in early childhood from the University of Memphis. The proud mother of one daughter and proud grandmother of two grandsons, she lives in Tennessee and New Jersey. For more information, visit www.fromthestarttraining.com

Acknowledgment

Dr. Scipio had the pleasure of teaching Sam Gilbert in Kindergarten Sunday school. They have cultivated an amazing friendship. He is now in the fifth grade. Sam is an avid reader, writer, and piano player who wants to make the world a better place for children.

He is very active in his church and participates in Lads to Leaders, a Christian leadership program. He is also an ambassador for the Tennessee Children's Home. He lives in Tennessee, with his dad, mom, brother, and sister. Sam provided insight from a child's perspective to enrich the companion guide *Let Me Teach You, Baby*.

Visit my website

www.fromthestarttraining.com

and download

2 FREE OFFERS

Top Ten Terrific Infant Tips

and

Top Ten Terrific Toddler Tips